M000308116

Endorsements

I couldn't put this book down! What an amazing story of trauma, frustration, and perseverance leading to eventual healing and deliverance. This story will encourage anyone who has struggled with chronic pain, trauma, unanswered prayer, hearing God's voice, and the timing of God's plan. It's a remarkable example of the supernatural power of forgiveness to heal and deliver. I was privileged to play a brief cameo role in this divinely directed drama that concluded with such victory. Read it right now—your breakthrough is waiting for you!

—Grant Mullen, MD, author of *Emotionally Free*

Pat has been a treasured friend and mentor for over two decades. She is one of those rare saints from whom the presence of God consistently flows. This book is similarly a treasure and a portal. Jettisoning my fear of cliché, I confess that, more than once, I found myself laughing (out loud) and wiping away welled-up tears. Inspiring and practical, biographical yet timeless, her words and her story left me both spiritually satisfied and thirsty for more. Like her, it's a treasure. So stop what you're doing, read this book, and prepare for the portal.

—Bill Campbell, pastor/missionary, France

To know Pat is to be drawn to living life more fully, more holy. Reading her story reveals the source of this power and makes me want to pursue freedom in Christ all the more.

—Mat Carson, director, Inspiro Arts Alliance, a
Ministry of Operation Mobilization

I have known and worked closely with Pat for many years. She is a dear friend, mentor, and colleague. I've seen God work powerfully in the lives of others and my own through Pat. Her wisdom, warmth, and love for people to experience real freedom in Christ are insatiable. She is the real deal—an ordinary hero living out God's extraordinary call.

—Dileep Ratnaike, arts catalyst, East Asia, Inspiro Arts Alliance

Collision: How I Found My Life by Accident, by my dear friend and colleague Pat Butler, is a disarmingly honest testimony of healing and deliverance through the power of Jesus Christ, the word of His truth, and the abiding presence of the Holy Spirit. It's an adventure of towering proportions, culminating in spiritual and physical freedom. Pat's compelling story offers monumental hope to anyone suffering from debilitating maladies that may have a spiritual source, highlighting the imperative of employing the biblical weapons of forgiveness, confession, and repentance.

—Bill Drake, director, Catalytic Ministries, OM International

I highly encourage you to read this story that reveals how God did a deep work of healing in Pat Butler, one of His beloved children. Having developed a close bond with Pat over many years beginning with our ministry together in France, my wife and I, along with our children, believe that Pat is truly a trophy of God's grace and power in life transformation. This book will benefit all who read it.

—Howard Moore, former GEM French field leader
and ministry team leader in Lille, France

Unexpected, undeniable, and completely transformational. Patricia Butler's *Collision* reveals the fullness of God's mercy when least expected. This book left me longing for more—more healing, more purpose, and more of God.

—Teresa Janzen, MEd, author, speaker,
teacher, and African explorer

Ready to take on a raw, transparent, and unexpected adventure filled with layers upon layers of surprises, emotions, and clarity? A journey from unspeakable despair to unwavering hope? Pat's story is the greatest gift and encouragement to any who need strength to believe in timely deliverance, godly purposes, and hope for unhealed wounds.

—Bonnie Chiang, founder of Bonivoyage Art

We're in a world where people suffer all kinds of ailments and are bound by evil. They question their predicaments with evil bondages and prolonged sickness. Those of faith seek a healing God, as He has promised healing to His children. Pat's testimony is valid. It sheds light on this God. It gives hope and strength to anyone looking for him. Without hesitation, I recommend *Collision, How I Found My Life by Accident*. It points people to faith, hope, perseverance, and trust.

—Ruth Kunguma, actress, scriptwriter, founder of Rubella Films

God works in unique ways for each of us. But as *Collision: How I Found My Life by Accident* powerfully describes, we can learn essential truths as we engage in another's narrative. Pat Butler's journey began with trauma and fear but ends in freedom and wholeness. She describes working at a local job before God thrust her into international missions. The journey's climax applies to every reader—the need to forgive. I encourage you to read Pat's story with an open heart and mind to the working of God in your life. This isn't a book to be read and put on a shelf. Revisit it regularly, asking God to search your heart for resentments and bitterness that require forgiveness. May each of us know the healing and freedom that results from choosing to forgive.

—Dr. Dianne B. Collard, author of *I Choose to Forgive: An Intimate Journey with God*, Europe Ministries director of ACT International, director of Montage International, director of Meraki*Connection

Collision might just collide with your comfortable way of thinking. We want to believe that God heals, but we often leave the door open in our minds "just in case He doesn't." Pat's story challenges our traditional view of Jehovah Rapha. In her testimony, you see a God who heals however He wishes but may also do deep spiritual work to release us from bondage. A quick read, but one that will challenge you to think of suffering and healing in ways you may never have.

—Beth Beutler, owner of H.O.P.E. Unlimited; author of *A Light for Your Path: Helping You Reflect on Each Chapter of the Bible*

Just as I was settling into a safer expression of faith, I started reading Pat's testimony—one I had heard before—and the Spirit stirred my imagination once again concerning the possibilities of the great, miracle-working God. The read is quick but substantial—an excellent combination! It will benefit all with an inquisitive mind and desirous heart, but I suspect the book will resonate most with the intuitive, the poet, the artist souls among us, as it puts on display a methodology of knowing God that, though fully rooted in Scripture, is not worked out in rational categories. Pat's story testifies to how God also works as an impressionist painter, revealing himself through the crafting of our ill-defined life experiences. With the Scriptures and the Holy Spirit as our guide, the blurred and muddy image becomes clear, beautiful, and revelational. As we step back from a too-close standpoint, we view with spiritual eyes the work of art that is the life of every child of God (Ephesians 2:10).

—Christopher Zito, author of *Doctrine and Experience: Caught in the Crossroads of Evangelical Spiritualities*

Collision

Collision

How I Found
My Life
by Accident

Patricia Butler

REDEMPTION
PRESS

© 2022 by Patricia Butler. All rights reserved.

Published by Redemption Press, PO Box 427, Enumclaw, WA 98022.
Toll-Free (844) 2REDEEM (273-3336)

Redemption Press is honored to present this title in partnership with the author. The views expressed or implied in this work are those of the author. Redemption Press provides our imprint seal representing design excellence, creative content, and high-quality production.

The author has tried to recreate events, locales, and conversations from memories, research, personal journals, ministry newsletters, and interviews with others. In order to maintain their anonymity, in some instances the names of individuals, some identifying characteristics, and some details may have been changed, such as physical properties, occupations, and places of residence.

Noncommercial interests may reproduce portions of this book without the express written permission of the author, provided the text does not exceed five hundred words. When reproducing text from this book, include the following credit line: "*Collision* by Patricia Butler. Used by permission."

Commercial interests: No part of this publication may be reproduced in any form, stored in a retrieval system, or transmitted in any form by any means—electronic, photocopy, recording, or otherwise—without prior written permission of the publisher/author, except as provided by United States of America copyright law.

Unless otherwise indicated, all Scripture quotations are from the Holy Bible, New International Version®, NIV®. Copyright © 1973, 1978, 1984, 2011 by Biblica, Inc.™ Used by permission of Zondervan. All rights reserved worldwide. www.zondervan.com The "NIV" and "New International Version" are trademarks registered in the United States Patent and Trademark Office by Biblica, Inc.™

Scripture quotations marked (NASB) are taken from the (NASB®) New American Standard Bible®, Copyright © 1960, 1971, 1977, 1995, 2020 by The Lockman Foundation. Used by permission. All rights reserved. www.lockman.org

Scripture quotations marked (TLB) are taken from The Living Bible copyright © 1971. Used by permission of Tyndale House Publishers, Carol Stream, Illinois 60188. All rights reserved.

Scripture quotations marked (MSG) are taken from THE MESSAGE, copyright © 1993, 2002, 2018 by Eugene H. Peterson. Used by permission of NavPress, represented by Tyndale House Publishers. All rights reserved.

Scripture quotations marked (KJV) are taken from the King James Version, public domain.

ISBN 13: 978-1-64645-319-1 (Paperback)
978-1-64645-318-4 (ePub)
978-1-64645-320-7 (Mobi)

Library of Congress Catalog Card Number: 2021925528

Dedication

To the One I met on a sailboat, on a floor in Vermont, and in the French Alps.

Acknowledgments

I praise God, Jehovah-Rapha, who heals all our diseases and leads us through unexpected journeys to do so.

Thanks to the team at Redemption Press, midwives to a book I didn't know I had in me—another unexpected journey. Shoutout to Athena Dean Holtz for the vision to host an online conference in a pandemic. To managing editor Dori De Vries Harrel, for her enthusiasm and annotated TOC on steroids. And to multitalented editor Karen Engle for your many layers of skill and excellent questions. I've become a better writer by working with you all.

To my Word Weavers Page 8 group: Thanks for questioning my original idea, for critiques, creative sparks, and valiant attempts to pronounce French. Your wisdom, prayer, and encouragement held me accountable and prodded me to dig more deeply.

Thank you to my Inspiro Arts Alliance tribe for your encouragement and prayer—and grace when I missed meetings.

I praise God for my rowdy Irish family for always cheerleading and never balking as I write about the family circus. Thank you! #loveyerguts

Thank you to those who financially contributed so quickly and generously to support the publication of *Collision* with prayers, affirmations, and encouragement. Without you, the project might well have skidded off a cliff.

Thanks to Donna, still my sidekick, who lived much of this story with me, jogged my memory, and pitched in on a moment's notice to read chapters or tackle administrivia.

Thanks to my beta readers who jumped in at the last minute when I switched gears.

Shoutout to Lisa Leach for helping me pinpoint the locus of the story and inspiring a new subtitle.

Thanks to my social media community for taking the polls, dropping emojis, and forwarding funny writer memes. I heart you.

Intercessors: Heaven alone knows the role you played and the reward awaiting you. Thank you.

Contents

Author's Note

Whoever finds their life will lose it, and whoever loses their life for my sake will find it.
Matthew 10:39

WELCOME! I'M SO GLAD YOU'RE HERE. I'VE PRAYED for you and worked carefully and prayerfully to find the right words and stories to tell you. My hope is to show you a view of God the Healer from my corner of the kingdom. I hope it will illuminate yours.

Like many people, I've wondered about healing. So many mysteries, endless questions. God chose a car accident as my tutorial. What I learned radically altered my life and understanding of healing and our Healer.

Collision opens with the accident that launched me into an unexpected journey. But this isn't a book about painkillers, physical therapy, and a long road to recovery—not entirely. I mention chiropractors, nurses, and orthopedists, but allies, mentors, and a sidekick take supporting roles. Only one IV drip appears, not attached to me.

My story starts with calamity but climaxes in a meta-collision between the kingdom of darkness and God's kingdom, which sparked transformation. I lost a lot but gained my life—abundant life—as Jesus promised (e.g., Matthew 10:39 and John 10:10).

As I developed the manuscript, the Spirit dropped surprising memories to include, the full impact of which I didn't grasp until I finished the book. I scoured journals, old prayer memos and newsletters, and others' memories to verify events. Many days ended in awe, worshiping God for his work in my life.

When we talk about spiritual realities, words fail. I've never heard God speak audibly and sincerely hope I've not put words in his mouth. All conversations with God in the text are my best attempt to translate what I perceived as his words to me. While I've primarily used the NIV (except where noted), I've adapted verses to how I talk with God, sometimes merging various translations. This is how God and I communicate. In our ongoing conversation, he is definitely more concise.

Discerning God's voice was essential at every step of the journey. It remains a fine art I practice. Thoughts, impressions, understanding, perceptions, and interpretations are mine. Confirming witnesses and circumstances will attest to my honest attempts at accuracy and sound theology. But I'm not a theologian. The texts I cite are not meant to be proof texts but breadcrumbs, puzzle pieces, pearls of great price gleaned from deep dives on the biblical theme of healing. In an ocean of pain, I found them in study, conversation with mentors, and in dreams. I invite you to join me in the ongoing quest to understand God and healing better, to serve him and the suffering.

The journey continues. All events and people in *Collision* are real, but I've changed some names and identifying details to protect privacy. If I inadvertently convey any misrepresentations in *Collision*, may the Spirit blow it away like chaff and replace it with substance and truth. He has the starring role in this story. I'm only the scribe, recording what I experienced, for the sake of his body, the church, and you.

Introduction

I love the LORD, for he heard my voice; he heard my cry for mercy. Because he turned his ear to me, I will call on him as long as I live.

Psalm 116:1–2

THERE IS A GOD WHO HEALS—BUT NOT ALWAYS AS WE expect.

His name is Jehovah-Rapha, and he hides treasures in darkness. This book is an invitation to seek these treasures, because this God also loves to reveal secrets and mysteries (Daniel 2:28).

Threshold guardians—gatekeepers who protect our cultural, religious, and medical institutions—fiercely defend these treasures. They may include family, friends, enemies, or our own fears and doubts. Potentially dangerous, they can also convert to allies.

At critical crossroads, guardians block our path, asking questions, testing our commitment:

- Why doesn't God heal?
- Why do we see some people healed and not others?
- When we don't see healing, do we lack faith? Is affliction our cross to bear, a discipline, or a thorn in our side?

These questions took on particular urgency after a car accident left me with severe spinal injuries and a "permanent" disability. The collision launched me into a twelve-year journey to find healing.

I searched with Job's tenacity. As far as I knew, I was guilty of no sin deserving such calamity. I wouldn't curse God, but I couldn't be satisfied with clichés, lazy answers, or veiled accusations. Friends showed up—as they did for Job—with speeches, advice, and beliefs that frustrated, angered, and confused me:

- It's not God's will.
- His grace is sufficient.
- This trial will build your faith.
- You are healed—just claim it.
- We're only healed in heaven.
- It's a mystery.
- You may be in sin.

Such responses rang hollow. People meant well or sincerely believed these statements (some of which are true). And like me, many were honestly grappling with the questions. These threshold guardians served a critical purpose—to drive me to God and probe his word, his thoughts, his ways. As with Job's friends, the speeches, advice, and beliefs of these guardians compelled me to declarations of faith, to refuse debate, and to hold out for God's answer.

While I pursued God, he orchestrated a global treasure hunt. He gave me a new identity and sent me to foreign countries, where I learned new languages. At each threshold crossing, he exposed enemies and trained my hands for battle. He surrounded me with allies and mentors and released new calls and gifts.

In time, doors opened, and the path cleared. God appeared in a whirlwind and healed me, as he did Job. And like Job, I repented and responded, "I read that you healed. Now I know you do" (Job 42:5, my paraphrase).

When we can't satisfy the threshold guardians, we may be denied or delayed access to healing. If we give up, we may forfeit it entirely. We also have an archenemy, who appears as an angel of light but is a counterfeit who steals, kills, and destroys.

How do we bypass the guardians and overcome the enemy of our soul?

Let me tell you my story. I'm not an expert on healing, but I can share the treasures I received in darkness. For this is more than the story of an accident or an invitation to find treasures. It's an appeal to persevere until you find life—abundant life.

Think of *Collision* as a map, a compass, a password book to help you unlock the secrets the threshold guardians defend. May you enter a true healing path and find the treasure you seek.

Above all, may you find Jesus, the Way, the Truth, and the Life—for the first time or in a new way. He is the Way into healing, the Truth about healing, and the One who promised abundant life. He is the Healer and wants to do more than heal you. He's after transformation. Listen for his voice as you read. Ask him your questions. Ask and keep on asking. He wants you to find him.

Prologue

Hear my cry, O God; listen to my prayer.
Psalm 61:1

FTER A CAR ACCIDENT WHEN I WAS THIRTY-FIVE YEARS old, I received a new identity: permanent disability. I rejected the label and begged God for healing over many years. After every imaginable treatment, with minimal improvement, doctors declared me stable. They discharged me with a disability rating and referred me to a psychiatrist to adapt to life with a disability. One depressing session with him, and I opted out.

As medical fees drained my savings, debts mounted, and I needed to replace my car—totaled in the accident. Medical insurance didn't cover alternative health treatments, so I used my credit cards. No claim would be reimbursed until the legal settlement, which took years.

People around me—even strangers—showered me with advice, welcome or not. Desperate, I tried every recommendation, learning what worked, what didn't, and what to ignore.

Some said God no longer healed but sent trials to refine us. His grace would be sufficient. Others urged me to have more faith, confess sin, or claim my healing. The Eeyores sidled up to me and sighed with downcast eyes.

Everyone had an opinion. None resonated with me. Eventually, I tuned the voices out or challenged those who suggested I lacked faith. If a treatment option came along, I researched it first, unwilling to try costly treatments with dubious results. I doubted myself in disability's strange landscape. Eager at first to try any option, I exhausted myself exploring every rabbit trail of treatment. I soon ran out of steam, money, and motivation and still wasn't healed. But if I stopped trying, I feared the alternative.

Two years after the accident, no healing had come in response to my prayers. Some suggested I accept this thorn in my side, like the apostle Paul, which sounded as depressing as the psychiatrist's advice. At least Paul had heard from God.

The breaking point came when my chiropractor said he could do nothing further. My spirit caved as another health care professional gave up on me. One last treatment option remained—costly, experimental, with no guarantee of success. I might be a candidate if I had the means to pay for it. (I didn't.)

In the evening, I poured out my complaint to God. He responded through one Scripture: "She had suffered a great deal under the care of many doctors and had spent all she had, yet instead of getting better she grew worse" (Mark 5:26).

The words arrested me. Her story matched mine—a woman desperate for healing, reaching out to Jesus. Hope flickered. A strong impression came over me to say "no" to further treatments. When I did, I felt a new journey had begun.

Trauma launches us into heroes' journeys. When I prayed for healing, I never imagined God's plan would include a twelve-year journey into art and missions. And that's just the external story. The internal story would include a journey into my heart to heal spiritual accidents—woundings and disabilities. For God's definition of healing went exponentially beyond mine—into transformation—and opened a new storyline.

The story begins in May 1985, on an ordinary evening in Hartford, Connecticut.

CHAPTER 1

Girl Moves to Hartford
1982–1985

All the days ordained for me were written in your book
before one of them came to be.
Psalm 139:16

WHEN I FIRST VISITED HARTFORD, THE CITY FASCI-nated me—especially the quirky home of Mark Twain, adjacent to Harriet Beecher Stowe's Victorian cottage. Wallace Stevens had also lived here, the insurance executive who walked to work composing poetry. For a book-loving wannabe poet, breathing the air of their city inspired me. As I walked its streets, admiring the eclectic architecture, I wondered about Hartford's contemporary literati. Where did they live? Could I enter their galaxy? The dream became a reality in April 1982, when I moved to Hartford with my friend Donna.

With a Sidekick

Donna and I met on Long Island, New York, in an animal hospital. I was one of two veterinary technicians on staff. Donna worked holidays and summers as a kennel worker while earning her veterinary technician degree. Small of stature and large of heart, Donna was a prankster with a hearty laugh and a sharp mind. We hit it off immediately. Even while wrestling animals for treatments or drawing blood samples, Donna and I tackled the deep questions of life, including spiritual matters.

Although we were born into Catholic families, we were now on different spiritual paths. My recent encounters with Jesus led me away from the religious scaffolding I grew up with and felt I'd outgrown. Donna pledged allegiance to the Baha'i religion, unknown to me at the time. While we worked, we compared the Bible and Baha'i teachings—elusive to me and probably to Donna too. But Eastern philosophies were trending, and we accepted one another while holding any reservations we had to ourselves.

After several years of working together, we felt the squeeze of Long Island's rapid development. The rising cost of living soon outpaced our salaries, so we shared housing to split expenses. As much as we loved the island, its increasing congestion grew claustrophobic. We talked about moving to upstate New York, near where we had both earned our college degrees. In 1980 we took the leap—with two cats, a dog, and a parakeet.

Unfortunately, the job market stagnated. Although we resisted veterinary science jobs as too low paying, we struggled to find steady work. Meanwhile, Donna's best friend and his wife moved to Hartford and encouraged us to join them—jobs were plentiful in the insurance capital of the world. To Hartford we drove for an exploratory visit.

Donna found work almost immediately with a financial start-up. Prospects looked promising for me too—Hartford clamored for office workers. Although the insurance industry didn't inspire me, Hartford's literary history did. With some high school office jobs in my background, I could start with temp work until something more meaningful presented itself.

In that first exploratory visit, Hartford's beauty captivated us, with its residential neighborhoods, small downtown, and broad boulevards. With plenty of parks, lakes, and rivers, Hartford would do just fine for our next adventure. We also found an apartment—Clemens Place, neighboring Mark Twain's quirky house. Donna had secured a job, and with an encouraging job market for me, we signed a lease.

To the Nutmeg State

During the upcoming Easter weekend, we drove back and forth from New York to Hartford, with packed cars and a van, finishing in time for a blizzard. "Welcome to New England," I sighed the next morning, opening the door to a fresh pile of snow.

The snow threatened to thwart my interview and Donna's first day on the job, but we didn't let snow stop us. We bundled up, shoveled for an hour, and dug out our cars in time for our commitments. Within a week, a commercial print company hired me as an administrative assistant. We survived the wait for our first paychecks and exhaled when they arrived. Now the fun could begin.

Our ethnically and culturally rich neighborhood offered a wide choice of coffee shops, restaurants, and boutiques. We could walk to many of them, as well as a movie theater and several churches. A bit further out was Elizabeth Park, with its lovely rose garden, and the YWCA, where I signed up for a pool membership. Missing Long Island's ocean, sound, and bays, I could at least swim—one of my favorite activities.

The diversity suited our roots growing up in New York City suburbs. Although I'd grown up on Long Island, my father's roots were in New England. I loved connecting to those roots as we explored the region's nooks and crannies. Our weekends filled quickly.

Few of Hartford's gems escaped our notice. We became regulars at Hartford's Civic Center, the South End's Italian bakeries, and the Wadsworth Atheneum—America's oldest art museum. The Noah Webster House, with its eye-catching colonial red, made a pretty sight in West Hartford. The city had an energy and beauty all its own, so refreshing after Long Island's congestion and upstate New York's poverty and isolation. The capital of Connecticut buzzed with young people like us making their mark.

We were living large in this historic city, but my life lacked a critical piece: a church home. Since my conversion, I had rarely enjoyed a satisfying spiritual community. Now it became top priority.

In a city full of historic churches, influenced by America's early revivals, I searched each weekend until I sensed a fit.

Calvary Church in West Hartford drew me in with its hospitality and thoughtful people. The church had just called a new pastor, Dr. Carl Abrahamsen, from Long Island. I joined as he did—a tall and lanky pastor with a familiar accent, who delivered power-packed sermons. And with him came the chance of a lifetime.

Shortly after I joined, Pastor A (as we called him) announced the church's participation in the upcoming Billy Graham New England Crusade and asked for volunteers. My hand shot up. Although I had grown up listening to Billy Graham, I never imagined I'd have an opportunity to work with him.

> **Although I grew up listening to Billy Graham, I never imagined I'd have an opportunity to work with him.**

Billy Graham Comes to Town

Billy Graham's training team arrived a year in advance, launching a beehive of activity to facilitate an eight-day crusade. Hartford's Christian community united, with the Catholic Church's support—over three hundred churches throughout Connecticut and western Massachusetts. Volunteers numbered over four thousand—clergy and laypeople alike. For one year, we trained, organized, and laid the groundwork for new believers and new members to enter our churches.

Every day, into the evening, and on weekends, volunteers arrived at Calvary—each one contributing whatever time they could to whatever task needed to be done. We prayed hard and worked diligently, motivated to contribute to a cause greater than ourselves. I signed up as a counselor. But hungry to soak up every aspect of the crusade, I attended as many meetings as possible. In my behind-the-scenes glimpses, I observed the humility, commitment, and professionalism of Graham's team. I wondered if I could work with them.

Excitement built through the year, mixed with exhaustion. Although I didn't know many people yet at Calvary, or they me, we forged lifelong relationships as we worked elbow to elbow each week. I met many local pastors and church leaders, broadening my view of Hartford's spiritual landscape.

And then Billy Graham came to town. The night before the crusades, he invited leaders, organizers, and volunteers for a night of encouragement and prayer. We sat in Hartford's cavernous civic center, an eight-day sprint awaiting us. And we were pumped. As I listened to Dr. Graham, I imagined how the civic center would fill the next evening. Or would it? New England was known as a spiritual wasteland. Yet Graham's historic 1957 New York crusade in Madison Square Garden had broken records.

As a child, watching Billy Graham on television mesmerized me. His words were simple but stirred something deep within me. When he issued his trademark invitation to come forward and commit to Christ, the crowds surged. What compelled them?

As a teenager, I scanned the television listings for Billy Graham crusades. Dad hated television but liked Billy Graham. If he knew a crusade was on, he'd tune in. And I'd be first on the floor, glued to the screen. The pattern never varied: songs and testimonies, a simple message, the invitation. And then thousands emptied from their seats to pray with Dr. Graham. What was the secret?

One night I had no questions but sensed the truth in Billy Graham's words. After the crusade, I went to my room in the attic, climbed into my window seat, and stared at the full moon. Although I didn't fully comprehend a commitment to Christ, I wanted to act on Dr. Graham's message. If I were attending a crusade, I'd have left my seat too. Instead, I prayed the sinner's prayer—the one he led thousands to pray. Four short lines seemed insufficient to God's magnitude, but I prayed them expecting to understand more in time.

The moon didn't blow up, and I didn't fall to the ground in a trance. But my spirit felt right, as if something had aligned. Maybe a four-line prayer meant nothing, but God heard my heart.

God in the Civic Center

Now, two decades later, I sat riveted in the Hartford Civic Center. Before me on the dais, the preliminaries were underway. Songs, testimonies, and announcements followed one after another, according to the familiar pattern. But I was impatient to hear Dr. Graham speak.

I scanned the crowd, my mind a screen with questions and impressions flickering like fireflies. What would happen tonight? Were people as antsy as me? Scared? Did the music engage the audience? Then the lights dimmed, and Dr. Graham took the pulpit to thunderous applause.

As he delivered his message, Dr. Graham's simplicity struck me again. His words certainly carried no power. Would they convince anyone or fall on deaf ears? When he issued his classic invitation to come forward and receive Christ, I held my breath in the silence that followed.

And then the magic unfolded. Thousands rose from their seats. They shuffled to the aisles, cascaded down the steps, and streamed forward, many in tears. They flooded the open space before the dais and waited patiently. Arms outstretched, heads bowed or looking around, they sang or prayed or stared ahead dazed. Some would later say they didn't know how they got there—they had had no intention of moving.

I sat and absorbed the scene before me. Dazed myself, I'd never experienced anything like this. Then I scrambled forward too. As a counselor, I wore a name tag and had a stack of cards ready to take contact info. My role was to look for someone without a tag and ask if they needed prayer, a church, or a visit.

Instead, I burst into tears and ripped my tag off. If we weren't shoulder to shoulder, I'd have been facedown of the floor. The sense of God's presence overpowered me.

A lady wearing a counselor tag approached and asked how she could pray for me. I confessed I was a counselor too—an overwhelmed one. Looking disappointed, she moved on. I wondered how anyone managed to carry on normally. The training team missed one thing: preparing volunteers for the possibility of experiencing God's presence in an unprecedented way.

As the evening concluded and the crowd gradually dispersed, I climbed into the bleachers and watched a few stragglers praying, wandering, or chatting. I couldn't wait for the second night.

Although I encouraged Donna to come if only for the historic moment, she declined. I kept praying for her that week, as I'd prayed all year. At work on Monday, I invited several friends I'd also prayed for—two came and went forward at Dr. Graham's invitation. By God's grace, I kept my act together for counseling the rest of the week.

The crusade made headlines every night, and Hartford was abuzz. The crowds swelled during the week, and by the weekend, Donna caved and joined me. Though she never moved from her seat, she listened intently. God was at work, but Donna's time had yet to come.

When the crusade ended, we counselors submitted our contact cards to the church. In exchange, we received a copy and a list of potential churches for each person, based on their location and denomination. The team had worked for a year to create this database—a labor of love. Each card felt like a sacred trust, and the team advised us to follow up within forty-eight hours.

And then the training team left. We dismantled the workroom at Calvary, and the churches disbanded. After a year of intense effort, Pastor A discharged us back to our ordinary lives. I descended from a spiritual mountaintop to my mundane work with a head full of wonder and a seed planted in my heart.

CHAPTER 2

An Accidental World
East Hartford, CT, May 1985

Heal me, LORD, and I will be healed.
Jeremiah 17:14

TWO DAYS AFTER THE CRUSADE ENDED, I WALKED along Farmington Avenue, one of Hartford's main arteries, under a canopy of cherry blossoms. After the long, harsh New England winter, Hartford's spring was a welcome sight. The songbirds returned, forsythia exploded along the highways, and music boomed from open windows. Cherry petals fluttered to the ground as I walked home from the pool in the clamor and bus fumes of rush-hour traffic. I thanked God for their beauty and my life in Hartford.

After a quick dinner, I hopped in my Honda Civic, opened the sunroof to the warm sunshine, and drove across the Connecticut River to East Hartford. A friend had invited me to learn about a business venture that capitalized on the Color Me Beautiful craze sweeping the city.[1] This trend popularized seasonal color analysis, aligning a woman's skin tone to her clothing and makeup. After a decade in veterinary science scrubs and lab coats, I wanted to jazz up my minimal business wardrobe. But I also craved some creativity in my life—a little side hustle into fashion and makeup would

---

[1] Carole Jackson's book *Color Me Beautiful* (New York: Ballantine Books, 1987) launched the trend and became an international bestseller. For more information, see https://www.colormebeautiful.com/.

be fun. I was on my way to meet the director.

My gratitude for financial stability with my job had already degenerated into restlessness. While I enjoyed the people and made friends, the work bored me. It trained me in office procedures and equipment (including newly emerging computers) but no creative outlet or inspiration.

At the sound of screeching brakes, my eyes darted to the rearview mirror. To my horror, it filled with a car's front grillwork. I braced for impact.

Until I found something more stimulating, I pursued the Color Me Beautiful trend to see where it might lead.

Collision

I arrived at my exit in East Hartford, slowed to ramp speed, and turned right onto a residential street. In those pre-GPS days, I scanned street signs for my next turn. At the sound of screeching brakes, my eyes darted to the rearview mirror. To my horror, it filled with a car's front grillwork. I braced for impact.

The collision whipped my head back, snapped the seat horizontal, and threw me backward. My knees caught on the steering wheel, tearing muscles through my thighs, lower back, up my spine, and into my neck and jaw. Flattened on the broken seat, I saw stars—literally and figuratively—through the sunroof. Treetops swirled as the Honda, propelled by the force of the crash, careened out of control down the street.

I struggled unsuccessfully to reach the brake pedal, to regain control of the car before it hit a tree, another vehicle, or a pedestrian. When the Honda (with manual transmission) finally bucked to a halt, I lay in shock but thankful—it could have been worse. I thought I might be injured but felt no pain. Could I sit up? Had anybody witnessed the collision?

Against a darkening sky, two faces appeared at opposite windows. A middle-aged moonfaced man peered in through black-framed glasses—the driver of the car. He knocked frantically on the passenger side.

"Are you okay?"

On my side, a blonde woman glared at him before turning to me.

"I saw everything and called the police," she said. "Are you okay?"

I nodded once, unable to speak, afraid to move. *Am I okay, Lord?* The woman stayed with me, sometimes answering muffled voices behind her. I stared through the sunroof at twinkling stars until flashing lights illuminated the night sky. A siren pierced the quiet street—the police.

Someone opened my door; a policeman checked me and disappeared. Voices drifted in and out of my stunned brain as he and another officer evaluated the scene. I tried to sit up and swing my legs out of the car door. Everything worked. No broken bones.

The blond woman hovered while my head spun. *Best not to stand yet,* I thought, holding my head in my hands, hunched over my knees. Anything bleeding? What did the car look like? I stared at the woman's flip-flops to focus on something, trying to concentrate. *Clear your head, Patto, clear your head.*

An officer's shoes appeared in my field of vision. He asked the woman a few questions, then her flip-flops vanished into the darkness. I wanted to cry out—to thank her—but couldn't find words. I forced myself to stand. After another head-spinning moment, I hobbled to the car's rear end. The collision felt like a minor train wreck but looked like a parking lot fender bender. *How is that possible?*

A policeman walked over to me with his clipboard and read with clinical detachment: "Fault is with the driver of the other vehicle . . . estimated speed 55 to 60 miles per hour" (well above the speed limit) . . . "Honda speed estimated at 25 and 30 miles an hour when hit."

I couldn't concentrate as he droned on, until he said "ambulance."

"No ambulance," I interrupted, trying to stand straighter. "Just give me a few minutes."

The policeman balked. The law required immediate medical attention for personal injury, he insisted, which meant a trip to the nearby emergency room.[2]

I compromised: I'd drive myself if he followed in his car. His scowl deepened, but he nodded. After steering me back into the broken seat, he turned for his car, lights still flashing.

The short distance to the ER proved a stiffer challenge than I expected, between the broken seat and manual transmission. I crawled along slowly, thankful no cars were on the road. As we arrived at the ER entrance, the policeman escorted me in, handed the nurse paperwork, and bid us good night. Keys and handcuffs jangled from his belt as he lumbered off.

Incident in the ER

The nurse checked me in and ushered me through swinging doors to a gurney in the hallway. She pointed to it and said, "We'll move you to a room as soon as one's available." Turning on her heel, she swooshed through the swinging doors. I stared after her, then at the too-high gurney. Climbing on stiffly, I hoped the wheels were locked.

The hallway was quiet and empty, with sickly green and yellow walls. A few yards down, a fluorescent light blinked. I lay there reliving the accident and the events leading up to it. *What if I'd taken another exit? Or had been five minutes late?*

I missed my evening appointment with the Color Me Beautiful lady—I'd have to call her. *How could I reach Donna? I'd need to find a doctor. And I'd miss work tomorrow.* I made a mental list. *Help, Lord. Heal whatever needs to be healed.*

My mind whirred on and on. *How seriously was I injured? What would happen next?* It was almost June. The rose garden at

---

[2] In Connecticut at the time, any accident resulting in personal injury automatically triggered a lawsuit.

Elizabeth Park would be in full bloom. Donna and I anticipated meeting friends for its free jazz concerts on Thursday evenings. By July, we'd be tubing down the Farmington River or driving to the coast. *How many summer plans would I have to cancel or postpone?*

The nurse came and wheeled me into a room, followed within minutes by a scruffy, slight, and anxious young man, one shoelace untied. He didn't identify himself—volunteer, intern, or orderly— and wore no lab coat or scrubs. After fumbling with a clipboard and paperwork, he asked a series of routine questions, then a creepy one:

"Are you sexually active?"

"No," I said, my guard up.

"When was the last time you had sex?" he continued, not looking up.

What? Anger flared.

He broke into a sweat. "How many times in the past few months have you—"

"What do these have to do with the accident?" I snapped.

Flustered, he collected his papers and fled. I lay on the gurney, scared and angry, prayers and questions swirling. *God help me. How long have I been here? What time is it? Heal me, Lord. Get me out of here. Let Donna know something's wrong.*

Finally, a doctor arrived, pulled a curtain around the gurney, and diagnosed me with whiplash—cervical and spinal. He fit me with a neck collar, handed me a written prescription, and discharged me. I wandered out through the deserted hallways and front entrance.

As I eased myself into the broken car seat, I wished the policeman were still around. Or Donna. Anyone. Even though I felt no pain, I was shaking, and the car seat was still broken. *Should I even be driving?* I wondered, mustering concentration. I turned the ignition key and pulled out slowly. *At least traffic will be light.*

Midnight Allies

I arrived home around midnight to the phone ringing—it was the Color Me Beautiful lady, wondering what happened. When

I told her, she recommended her doctor and lawyer. I grabbed a napkin from the kitchen and jotted names and numbers. As I hung up, adding the napkin to my police report, prescription, and medical papers, Donna arrived. She dropped her bag, keys, and mail on the table, took one look at me, and asked, "What happened?"

As I told her, Donna sorted through my napkin and papers, tapping them into a neat pile.

"I'll take tomorrow off and drive you around," she said. In an unexpected journey into an accidental world, Donna was my first ally.

CHAPTER 3

Whiplash
1985–1987

*I will stand at my watch and station myself on the
ramparts; I will look to see what he will say to me, and
what answer I am to give to this complaint.*
Habakkuk 2:1

OUR FIRST TASK THE NEXT MORNING WAS TO COAX
the broken Honda over to a local auto body shop. Then
Donna chauffeured me to the orthopedist, a gruff man
with no discernible bedside manner but a reputation as Hartford's
best. He confirmed cervical and lumbar whiplashes and added
"lumbar sprain and muscle strain from knees to jaw." The simple
neck collar I wore seemed a feeble solution for these injuries, but
I still felt no pain. How long did shock last? The doctor answered
my questions in a bored monotone and dismissed me with a second
prescription.

We drove across the river to East Hartford legal offices to meet
my new lawyer. A tall, sour-faced man, also with no discernible
bedside manner, strode in and introduced himself. He fanned
out paperwork before me, outlining the process and timeline for
a personal injury lawsuit. When the doctors discharged me from
medical care, my case would begin. In the meantime, the lawyer
advised, I should keep track of all expenses. A lawsuit could take
years. *Years?* I took notes as I entered this grim new world. Sobered
by its realities, my natural optimism faltered. I envisioned medical

bills, administration, and legalese clogging my life for the foreseeable future—in the company of a surly lawyer and a gruff doctor.

Back over the river to West Hartford, we stopped by my office for my paycheck. Donna ran in—I was out of steam, embarrassed by the collar, and ached all over. Before circling home, we stopped at the pharmacy for my prescriptions. Once home, I popped the pills and lay down, sensing a seismic wave about to hit. I hoped the drugs would kick in before it arrived, but they didn't. Instead, intense pain pinned me to the bed as the last layers of shock wore off, and my body reacted to the trauma. For days, I lay in bed drugged and immobilized.

The Road of Trials

Life now revolved around drugs, medical visits, and adjustments to living with debilitating pain. The next dose of painkillers never came soon enough, and I prayed for grace to make it through the hours between doses. The hours turned to days, weeks, months.

I learned about hot packs, ice packs, massage and mineral baths, chiropractors and physical therapy, knee and neck pillows, hacks, and gadgets to manage pain. As I tracked receipts, appointments, prescriptions, and insurance claims, paperwork piled up. On my employer's advice, I filed for disability. As the weeks progressed, I kept my manager updated on my situation.

To distract myself from pain, I read, watched movies, did puzzles, or lay in bed staring at the ceiling, listening to music. I pondered all I'd seen and heard at Dr. Graham's crusades—the multitudes moving forward, the worship, the messages. The energy and exhilaration of the crusade year spotlighted the discontent in my job. I wondered about working in his organization and traveling the world.

The auto shop called to pronounce the Honda dead—its axle bent in the collision. As soon as I could drive, I'd need a new car. My brother Tom, the family caretaker, offered me one he planned to junk. Maybe it would hold me till I could afford something better. He drove it up from Long Island, no doubt listening to Scott

Joplin, Leon Redbone, and Jelly Roll Morton. Everyone needs a brother Tom.

A Snail's Pace

My first milestone was a swim—or an attempt. After a few sweet minutes of moving limbs through water and floating weightless, I felt like I'd run a marathon. But the victory was exhilarating. I persisted for weeks until I could manage a few laps. Swimming decompressed my spine and cleared my head. As muscles strengthened, pain decreased, at least temporarily. When I discovered a massage therapist at the pool, I scheduled appointments after swimming. I hoped she could unknot the chronic spasms along my spine.

By the end of summer, I attempted work, calling my manager to alert him. He encouraged me to start slowly, at whatever pace I could handle, and never mentioned any inconvenience. Starting with an hour or two a day, I hoped to build strength and stamina to work full-time again. My coworkers cheered when I walked in the door and remained flexible, supportive, and generous with me through the months ahead.

Work became a lifeline. I had a goal each day and an income, however meager, to pay bills. Since I needed no extra stress, I welcomed the monotony. And the social interaction compensated for disability's isolation. Above all, work represented a return to normalcy.

The biggest challenge was the volume and physicality of the work. Our office was attached to the printing plant and warehouse. My duties involved servicing the sales team by pulling printing samples from the warehouse and shipping them to sales reps. Since they called in constantly, I knew every aisle of inventory, all the storerooms, and the shipping center. They might as well have been Mount Everest or the North Pole for my ability to reach them now.

If I'd worn a Fitbit, I'd have clocked thousands of steps in my previous life. Now I limped around the plant and begged favors of coworkers. Within an hour or two, I was done—wiped out by fatigue and spasms—and went home to sleep off the effort.

The stress of trying to perform did nothing to improve my rehabilitation or mood. Although the quality of my work didn't suffer, the quantity plummeted. Rarely working more than a few hours a day, I arrived late and left early, maneuvering around spasms, fatigue, migraines, pinched nerves, and medical appointments. Everyone remained gracious, but as my absenteeism rose, the handwriting was on the wall. I could no longer manage this job.

A Sin, a Cross, or a Thorn?

I also couldn't ride in a car for long without triggering spasms. Couldn't wash the kitchen floor or carry anything over ten pounds. Couldn't dance, hike, or make it up some stairwells. Playtime with my nieces and nephews became problematic. All their bending, jumping, and swinging challenged my limitations. Even a too-tight hug hurt. Unless we read or watched a movie, their energy exhausted me.

Though I refused to identify myself as disabled, I now viewed the world through the eyes of a disabled person. As I navigated public spaces, I calculated how to open heavy doors or climb stairs without handrails. I habitually scouted for parking spaces, chairs, and beds to find ones to suit my needs, feeling terribly selfish and picky.

Donna remained faithful. As my finances failed, she bailed me out on rent, utilities, and groceries. As my ability shrank to simple household chores, she handled the scrubbing, vacuuming, and mopping. We alternated cooking during the week, although Donna frequently proposed dinner at the corner Indian or Vietnamese restaurant—her treat. On special occasions, she baked a tray of lasagna or stuffed shells. Thank God for those carb-busting meals—I'd lost quite a bit of weight.

I still lived for the next dose of painkiller, praying for endurance, grace, and healing. Severe migraines blindsided me, flattening me for hours. With each visit to the orthopedic doctor, he expressed more skepticism than concern, more snarky comments than hope.

After two years of pursuing every imaginable medical treatment, I saw minimal improvement. Although I didn't realize it, I had sunk into depression. The doctors discharged me with a disability rating of 10–15 percent. They referred me to a psychiatrist to adapt to a new normal, but after one depressing session with him, I opted out. At thirty-five years old, I refused the verdict of "lifetime disability" and cried out to God.

But I'd prayed for two years and heard nothing. Well-intentioned church people quoted Paul: God's grace would be sufficient for this thorn in my side (2 Corinthians 12:7-9). Their words didn't resonate. *Paul's answer,* I thought, *not mine—at least, not yet.* I wanted allies who would seek God with me, not lapse into clichés. Clichés were no match for the realities of living with a disability. I interpreted God's silence as encouragement to keep asking—he hadn't said no—so I persevered.

The passages I clung to spoke of Jacob wrestling, Paul pleading, a widow persisting (Genesis 32:22–28; 2 Corinthians 12:8–10; Luke 18:1–8). Job would die before he gave up hope in God (Job 13:15). Jacob received a blessing, Paul accepted God's word about his thorn, and the persistent widow received justice. Their stories resonated with me,

Throw me a bone, Lord! Am I being punished for sin? Is this a thorn in my side? My cross to bear?

so I took my stand, like Habakkuk, waiting for my word from God. *Throw me a bone, Lord! Am I being punished for sin? Is this a thorn in my side? My cross to bear?*

Determined to find solutions, I investigated alternative, experimental, even questionable treatments. Anger and depression haunted me—more than I knew. But despite my efforts, I never broke the pain barrier. After two years, I still had to lie down an hour or more a day to relieve pressure on discs and nerves. Each month I spent a day or a week in bed with severe spasms or debilitating headaches. Something had to change.

CHAPTER 4

New York, New York
1987

I cry out to God Most High, to God, who vindicates me.
Psalm 57:2

As I STRUGGLED TO REGAIN A WORK ROUTINE, I dreamed about my next job. Whatever I applied for, I didn't want to lie or try to conceal a disability. My absenteeism would expose me soon enough. With more time, I hoped for more stability, less pain, and less absenteeism. But how long would my current employer tolerate my reduced hours? And how should I present myself to a potential employer?

I pulled out my resume and reviewed it. It listed a patchwork quilt of jobs—from veterinary science to retail to office administration. How would an employer evaluate it? How could I make it more appealing? While formulating some explanations, I updated the resume.

Where did I want this new job? A commute of any length would jeopardize my carefully orchestrated appointments with doctors, the chiropractor, and my massage therapist. Along with swimming, these critical pieces kept me functional. I wanted something local, walking distance even, and circled the area on the map I'd be willing to travel.

Most importantly, what did I want to do? What was my niche—the one people talked about, the work I was born to do? God had a purpose for me, but what was it? *High time I figured it out.*

I thought about job counseling. It probably cost too much, but I hadn't let money stop me from pursuing a healing path. Why start now? I could at least research costs while seeking God for provision. Until he healed me or my employer replaced me or I knew my direction, I'd stay put in my current job.

Arts or Mission?

I found a career counselor around the corner from our apartment in one of Hartford's historic brownstones. We met for an initial consultation to discuss the process, goals, and costs. As I entered a lawyerly office, I noticed the counselor's collection of model planes. They were hard to miss—one hung suspended from the ceiling, and framed prints lined the walls. Smaller models perched on the counselor's desk and credenza.

"I see you like planes," I remarked, and he nodded, New England reserve intact. He shuffled papers on his desk, then dug out my file and a clipboard and pointed to two club chairs where we'd sit. With a coffee table between us, we settled in, and he studied my file.

"My father served in the air force," I offered, "and his brother sketched biplanes." Was that a half smile I detected under his mustache?

"Hot air balloons too," I added as he rearranged papers and clipped them to his clipboard. *This is getting awkward.*

When the counselor finally engaged, he complimented me on achieving the first goal of a job interview: create rapport with your potential employer and build relationship. *No problem,* I thought. *I'm a relational beast.*

Apparently, the counselor designed the awkward opening to evaluate my personality and social skills. As he sized me up, he zeroed in on the key question. What did I want in a job other than a paycheck? *Ah yes. My niche.*

"That's why I'm here," I replied.

He outlined a process designed to find my goal, which sounded perfect. After discussing a payment plan, I signed on the dotted line.

A series of appointments followed for interviews, a skills inventory, personality and aptitude tests, and homework assignments. Within weeks, we established some broad categories of interest to target. Then the counselor sent me to the library with a list of reference materials to refine my search.

Life before Google meant hours in Hartford's dusty downtown library. Under its musty windows, I pored over thick volumes I never knew existed. Comparing jobs to markets to salary ranges, I combed through possibilities. Two areas repeatedly turned up: the arts and missions. The arts didn't surprise me since my father was an artist. But he had discouraged me from becoming one in high school, saying, "Keep the arts as a hobby but find a job that pays." Since we grew up with the financial reality, I believed him. But missions? Way too scary.

I kept searching the listings, but the more I searched, the more "arts" and "missions" popped up. I focused on the arts, thinking I could easily enter through administration. Not the most appealing position, but a foot in the door to a new industry. *And if the arts don't work out,* I thought, *I'll think about missions.*

The career counselor suggested I interview people in various arts sectors to find a position I liked. I thought of Dad. As one of the movers and shakers in the mid-century modern movement, he played a pioneering role in a leading commercial interior design firm. He enjoyed considerable success and survived crushing financial setbacks in a volatile industry. On occasion, Dad brought my older brother Paul and me into his Manhattan office from our little fishing village of Oyster Bay.

From Bay to Metropolis

On a train jammed with commuters, we lumbered westward on the LIRR. I recognized a few neighbors in the crowd, and Dad quickly found his buddies. While he chatted with them, my brother at his elbow, I stared out the window at the highways, towns, and train stations, wondering what it would be like to live in each place.

Finally, our smelly, swaying, rattling train screeched to a halt in a cavernous underground station, a dungeon filled with graffiti and trash—Penn Station.

Exploding out of the train, we stampeded up stairs and escalators to streets lined with towering skyscrapers. In the blare of horns surrounding us, we scurried through the concrete jungle. I ran like a gazelle fleeing a predator, my eyes riveted on Dad. But when we entered his skyscraper on 320 Park Avenue, my jaw dropped.

From the cacophony of the streets, we twirled through a revolving door into cathedral-like space, silent except for muted voices and the whoosh of elevator banks. Marble columns drew my eyes from the atrium to men and women bustling about on upper floors, bordered with glass walls. Escalators transported figures with briefcases up and down the levels like angels ascending and descending Jacob's ladder. My eyes followed them, and I wondered, *Were we even allowed here?*

Dad herded us to the elevators. We entered one crammed with men in fedoras and a cloud of smoke. With stomach-lurching speed, the elevator rose through dozens of floors and opened its doors to a new world: Knoll Associates.

Dad showed us into his office, introducing us to his coworkers along the way. A design beehive hummed around us, the air electric with ideas. Architects and designers huddled around model interiors, discussing the placement of color swatches, cut-out furniture, and fake lichen.

In a quieter corner, Dad's office gleamed white in the sunlight pouring in from floor-to-ceiling windows. He set down his fedora and briefcase while we gaped out the windows at towers of glass and steel boxes—midtown Manhattan. Miles above the street (judging by my vertigo), we stared at miniature taxis, buses, and people.

"Want to see a showroom?" Dad asked.

"Yes!" we exclaimed, though I'm not sure either of us knew what he meant. We rode the elevator again, dropping down a few floors until the doors opened, and I gasped.

Under a black loft ceiling, otherworldly light fixtures shimmered. Gold and orange fabrics gleamed from walls and furniture, artfully positioned against neutral woods and floors. As far as my eyes could see, open showrooms spanned an entire skyscraper floor, with plants dotting the landscape. Awestruck, Paul and I wandered into the immensity while Dad consulted with the big people.

When he concluded his business, Dad waved us over and led us back to the elevators and down to his office. Before excusing himself for a meeting, he rummaged around for drawing templates, fabric swatches, and fake lichen, tossing them on his drafting table.

"Design your own space," he suggested, adding mat knives and foam core. We dove in, all thumbs.

At lunchtime, Dad reappeared and kicked us to the curb—literally. With another stomach-dropping descent on the elevator, he handed us some money and pointed to a curbside hot dog cart. He gave us a few tips on what to see in the neighborhood and how to orient ourselves if we lost our way: "Remember, it's a grid." With a stern admonition to be back by five o'clock, he waved goodbye and disappeared into Knoll's cathedral.

These early adventures instilled in me a love of art, design, adventure, and architecture.

My brother bolted in freedom. I darted after him, afraid Manhattan would swallow me alive. Although I couldn't keep up, we somehow managed to find each other and Dad's office before five o'clock.

These early adventures instilled in me a love of art, design, adventure, and architecture. With Dad's confidence that we could manage New York, I developed a taste for exploration and a good sense of direction. I loved roaming Manhattan and paid close attention to my surroundings. Later, when I moved to Europe, I prowled its cities—map in hand and a knack for finding public bathrooms.

While enjoying each city's charms, I kept my bearings and stopped at curbside food trucks for meals.

From Hartford to Manhattan

Now I set out to explore Hartford's art and design sector, remembering Dad's office. Could I find anything approaching his invigorating world in my adopted city? Maybe not, but Hartford's small size meant no noisy trains, less pollution, and no long commutes. I called Dad for advice, expecting him to discourage me from the arts again. But he had successfully provided for a large family and his widowed mother. If he managed, why not me? Maybe he had some ideas.

Dad did indeed have an idea: resource director in a design firm. In this position, I would investigate new design products, meet with sales reps, attend design shows, and propose solutions to the design staff. He offered to arrange a meeting with the resource director in his new firm, a design studio near Greenwich Village. I jumped at the opportunity.

After buying a new outfit, I traveled into Manhattan from Hartford and walked over to Dad's office. He introduced me to his resource director, and I spent the morning with her, listening, asking questions, meeting sales reps. Another glimpse of the New York design world mesmerized me. My head raced, brimming with ideas.

After lunch with Dad, I headed home, outlining a potential position description on the train. I then worked with the career counselor to finalize it into a proposal with a letter of introduction, targeting Hartford's top design firms. The counselor coached me on the informational interview, calculated to create a relationship with potential employers. When I was ready, I mailed the letters.

It took patience, persistence, follow-up, and a dozen interviews. But as I moved through the process, I gleaned information about needs, salaries, and staffing gaps. I noted office space, personalities, and staff dynamics. When I finally landed a position, I knew all the design firms in Hartford and some of their vendors. In a small city, this knowledge proved invaluable.

Advent Design, a woman-owned firm, accepted my proposal for resource director. I started in September 1987, over two years since the accident. With the change, I hoped to find more healing—and prayed my back would behave.

CHAPTER 5

A Crisis and a Click
1987–1989

Once again David inquired of the LORD.
1 Samuel 23:4

ADVENT DESIGN EMPLOYED A DOZEN FEMALE DESIGNers—and me. In this unique, creative environment, I found my niche and my tribe. Highly motivated, I added more strategies to function normally. To maximize strength, energy, and health, I stuck to a healthy diet and swam laps at the pool. Standing for any length of time increased pain, so I abandoned heels for flats and sneakers. A draft could trigger a neck spasm, so I dressed in layers and wore scarves.

At the end of each workday, I drove to my other tribe: swimmers, chiropractors, and massage therapists. With their care, I moved less like a robot but with a limited range of motion. I disguised or managed pain long enough to establish reliability with my employers and staff. It would be a year before back issues kept me from work.

While I thrived at Advent Design, I flourished spiritually at Calvary Church. The teachings were excellent. The church's health, hospitality, and family atmosphere combined to form my faith. Pastor A took me under his wing, and the elders took a special interest in me and other young people. Into the goodness flowed guest speakers, missionaries, and internationals. Calvary created a safe environment for others, and I invited everyone I knew.

Through a series of miraculous events, God drew Donna into the kingdom. We invited family, friends, and neighbors to her baptism. Before long, some of my cohorts at Advent braved an invitation for a Sunday morning or some event. One coworker had a dream about me. Friends from the print shop who had come to faith through the Billy Graham Crusade also crossed the threshold. In our weekly prayer meetings, we prayed for each person I invited. As we prayed, we witnessed one conversion after another. The pew I sat in filled to overflowing and was nicknamed "Pat's Pew."

Another joy was the migration of family members from New York to Connecticut. Paul and Maureen arrived first, trailing four kids. My sister, Mary, and her husband, Brian, followed and soon added two more children to the tribe. Finally, after Dad retired, our parents relocated, leaving three brothers in Oyster Bay—Tom, Allen, and Peter.

We lived close enough to each other to take turns entertaining. Our Irish hooleys included stories, music, dance, and the occasional fiddle player drinking boilermakers. Mom plied us with soda bread, and my sister perfected scones and treacle bread. On St. Patrick's Day—coincidentally my birthday—we broke out the Guinness (although our grandmother had a wee nip year-round). And after the corned beef and cabbage, we toasted with Bailey's Irish Cream. By the grace of God, we all escaped alcoholism.

Despite ongoing pain and disability, these were happier days. But in the joy, a crisis brewed.

Running on Empty

My low salary couldn't meet medical costs, which were draining my savings, and it was time to replace the car. The orthopedist refused to renew my prescription for painkillers, citing the risk of addiction. When he hinted that I was prolonging treatment in pursuit of a larger settlement, I changed doctors. Between doctors, I stocked up on over-the-counter painkillers. Ignoring the recommended dosage, I swallowed whatever I needed to relieve pain.

I started acupuncture—a disaster. Each needle pierced like a knife as if hitting a nerve. The acupuncturist had no explanation, and I had no desire to continue.

I persevered with my chiropractor until he told me he could do nothing more except relieve pain (as if that wasn't enough). But he had researched a new syndrome, chronic fibromyalgia, which explained some of my symptoms. A costly and experimental procedure that required hospitalization might relax the chronic knots of spasms in my back and neck. The treatment sounded gruesome with no guarantee of success.

The chiropractor suggested consulting with doctors to investigate this new option and closed our appointment by handing me an invoice. Could I start paying down my debt? With no means to do so—or pay for the proposed treatment—I slumped home in defeat.

That evening, I crawled into bed, Bible in my lap, and poured out my complaint. Even though God remained silent on healing, he still hadn't said no. His care and guidance were evident through job counseling and my new job. I hadn't gone bankrupt, and my junk car endured far longer than expected. God was providing. Why wasn't he healing?

Stories from David's life intrigued me during this period, especially ones that described how he strengthened himself in the Lord (1 Samuel 30:6). Whether fleeing King Saul or facing battles with the Philistines, David "inquired of the LORD" (1 Samuel 23:1–5, 9–11). He asked simple questions and received straightforward replies. How did God respond? The Scriptures don't give details, so I imitated David by asking simply, *Should I accept this treatment or not?*

My Bible was open to Mark's Gospel. The first words I read arrested me: "She had suffered a great deal under the care of many doctors and had spent all she had, yet instead of getting better she grew worse" (Mark 5:26).

Faith and hope collided with despair. The woman's story matched mine, but unlike her, fear paralyzed me. What if I refused the treatment? I might miss healing. But how could I pay for it?

> **Faith and hope collided with despair. The woman's story matched mine, but unlike her, fear paralyzed me.**

Her story suggested I'd find my answers not in the medical system but with Jesus. Following her example, I reached out one more time, asking Jesus for wisdom and direction. I wanted no more treatments.

What would Jesus do? I didn't know but affirmed out loud, "You won't fail me. Something will happen."

A shadow lifted, and my mind cleared. Strength poured in, and fear vanished. With no idea what would happen next, my spirit relaxed. I fell asleep like a rock.

Uncle Leo and the Watch Case

As I loosened my grip on seeking medical solutions, another light flared in my soul, with increasing insistence: What about missions? I turned my attention to it.

As in many Irish Catholic families, we had regular interaction with clergy. The parish priests and nuns taught us, and some became friends. We observed up close and personal the humanity behind their mysterious robes and incantations. The only scandal to hit our parish was a love affair between a priest and a nun, although other scandals surfaced in later years. But in our family circle, no one behaved inappropriately.

We had two missionaries in our heritage—both now deceased. I never knew my Aunt Bridget, who entered a convent at an early age in Dungarvan (Co. Waterford), Ireland. An excellent musician and music teacher, she later emigrated to Australia, where she died. Uncle Leo, a Jesuit priest, lived and worked in education for forty years in Jamaica, the West Indies. He entered my life when I was quite young.

Mystery surrounded our first meeting. An uncle I didn't know existed would pay us a rare visit—rare because he was a missionary, whatever that meant. Before he arrived, Dad mowed the lawn while Mom cleaned and baked. They smiled knowingly and answered ambiguously as we plied them with questions. But their excitement implied someone like Santa Claus was coming to town. Gifts and blessings would abound—for he was a missionary.

On the day of his arrival, we stared out the windows, and Dad paced near the front door. I wondered what a missionary looked like. When Uncle Leo walked in, a jaunty hat on his head, his large, square frame filled the door. My brothers jumped up and down, my father vigorously pumped his hand, and Mom beamed with pride. Having a missionary in the house was a badge of honor—one in the family surely meant bonus points. I watched from the side, wondering if I would like this mystery man of God.

The chatter and joy subsided as Uncle Leo noticed me staring at him. He walked over but stopped a few steps away. As if honoring an important dignitary, he waited while I checked him out.

"And who is this?" he asked with a kindly twinkle and enchanting voice—just as I imagined Santa Claus.

My parents introduced me—the lone sister in a gaggle of three rambunctious brothers. (Mary had yet to arrive to help me survive them.) Uncle Leo bowed slightly, offered his hand, and invited me to sit with him on the sofa. I felt like a princess—the missionary had singled me out! As if Mom, Dad, and my brothers had vanished, we sat and chatted.

Uncle Leo had arrived empty-handed and distributed no brightly wrapped toys. But pulling treasures from his pockets, he presented me with a watch case. Now empty, it hinted at secrets. With no visible gift, I wondered why he showed it to me. Another child might have been disappointed and questioned Uncle Leo.

But when he demonstrated how the box opened and closed with a satisfying click, we both laughed. The gift was in the sound and the complicity of a shared joke. For the rest of my life, the click remained with me, recalling Uncle Leo's warmth and an inner resonance by which I recognized God's voice.

Uncle Leo told me I could keep the case (I noted, as children do, he offered no one else a gift). His benevolence prompted an equally generous response in me—to not gloat over my brothers.

Each visit with Uncle Leo marked me differently but always included his joy, attentiveness, and unusual gifts. By far, his greatest impact was spiritual. When he talked to me, he treated me like an adult who could understand deep things. And I wanted to understand "missionary."

"What do you do?" I asked him one day.

"I teach schoolchildren like you."

"What do you teach them?" I persisted. *Why couldn't he teach in our school?*

"About God."

God in Grandma's Bedroom

I already knew God was the most important person in the world, even if he was invisible and lived to infinity. We'd meet him when we died. I wanted to meet him sooner, but on that point, adults were cryptic—even Uncle Leo. When I asked him how to get to heaven (which sounded much better than hell), he answered, "Through God."

I moved Uncle Leo to a new category, which included exactly one other person: my grandmother. She talked to God every day, at precisely 4:00 p.m., behind closed doors in her bedroom. One day, after a prolonged siege to wear her down, she granted me entrance, under pain of expulsion if I disturbed her.

I solemnly promised to behave and followed Grandma into the holy of holies, glancing around for a glimpse of God. She knelt by the bed, her prayer book before her, and closed her eyes. Lips moving, she was soon lost to me. I watched silently—thinking, *So this is prayer.*

With her eyes closed, I was free to move about. I roamed her room, inspecting her curios and photos, checking on her constantly in case God appeared. Finally, I knelt next to her and stared into her face. She was communicating with someone—I sensed a presence. *This must be God.* I hoped to meet him when I grew up.

By the look on Uncle Leo's face when he talked about God, I guessed he knew God too. I thought he had the best job in the world to teach people about God and hoped he would teach me one day. But Uncle Leo's visits ended a few years later when he died. I missed his visits with his gifts of kindness, presence, and conversation. But the seeds he planted in my soul now pushed through the soil as a persistent nudge to missions—God's call to the next generation of Butlers.

CHAPTER 6

Angels and Burning Bushes
1989

*For he will command his angels concerning you to guard
you in all your ways.*
Psalm 91:11

U P UNTIL THIS POINT IN MY CHURCH LIFE, I USUALLY
skipped missionary meetings as optional extras. When one
church friend challenged my attitude, I pleaded guilty and
started attending with her.

Some missionaries bored me with their blurry slides (back in the
day) and monotone presentations. I listened anyway and wondered
how such ordinary people landed in such adventurous lives. They
didn't look like Indiana Jones. Their clothes and hairstyles were often
dated, and they wore thick glasses. In my arrogance I thought, *If
I were a missionary, I'd make better fashion choices and create better
slide shows.* (Within years, I added graphic design, communications,
and public speaking to my missionary skill set.)

As missionaries described their countries, I wondered what
life was like for them. I imagined myself in a hut, enduring wicked
climates, eating locusts, snakes, and eyeballs. Cultures fascinated
me. Fueled by *National Geographic*, my father's heady design world,
and Manhattan's melting pot, my imagination soared. Dad often
brought internationals home for a meal. We listened to their stories,
heard strange accents, and received exotic gifts.

Now I brought missionaries home for a meal and sought out people of other cultures. With missionaries, our conversations usually revolved around their work, a quirky local custom, or the cultural slant on a theological point. When I asked about calling, they evaded. Why? Did they feel they had a call? Some said yes. Others thought a call wasn't necessary.

I also noticed a hesitation when I asked missionaries about spiritual warfare. What were their secrets? The stories I knew from Catholic lore were explicit, fantastical stories, hard to believe. The missionaries I met with talked in the abstract about oppression, temptation, and deception. I wanted details.

I read classic missionary biographies. In particular, Amy Carmichael, Elisabeth Elliot, and Gladys Aylward strongly impressed me. I admired their humble, risky, fearless faith. How did they acquire such faith? How could I? These missionaries belonged to times past. What did missionaries look like now?

International Sensibilities

I had an example at Calvary, John and Jessie Barney, retired missionaries to Africa. They became my living biography on all things missional. As lively and joyful a couple as anyone I knew, the Barneys carried a wealth of experience and practical wisdom. On Sundays, they often invited singles over for lunch, and Donna and I usually accepted. While I enjoyed the singles, I kept one ear tuned to the Barneys. Listening to their comical stories, I also gleaned important insights. Jessie's Kenyan-American fusion cuisine, served in Kenyan baskets, delighted the eyes and taste buds. During cleanup in the kitchen, I plied her with questions on recipes and missions.

Donna and I involved ourselves in International Student Ministries at nearby University of Hartford. We hosted students, offering friendship and practical advice as they adapted to American life. My usual questions hovered as we learned about their lives. *What is their country like? Could I live in their climate? Eat that food?*

I also participated in the International Women's Circle, a civic group that met at the church. This group organized monthly meetings for international women. After a potluck brunch, we facilitated workshops—everything from language and culture to completing government forms. In exchange, the women brought their traditional foods and taught us about their culture. I loved these rich exchanges. As a child, I wanted to visit every country in the world. Now God was bringing the world to me.

As my international sensibilities grew, a missionary spoke at Calvary who rocked my world. He concluded his presentation with a charge to the church: ask God to call a missionary from our congregation. I gulped. Was it my imagination, or did the lights dim and a spotlight beam on my head?

Red Light, Green Light

Our weekly prayer meetings now included this prayer—asking God to call a missionary from Calvary. Each week, I swore a spotlight shone on me. With my eyes closed and head bowed, I hoped no one noticed.

But I took the risk of confiding in the Barneys and a few close friends. Did my draw to missions indicate a call? Everyone suggested I talk with Pastor A, who I'd been avoiding. If I asked him, he'd grill me to see if I meant business. Missions remained a scary, overwhelming proposition. How serious was I? More importantly (and more terrifying), how serious was God? But my friends were right. I called Pastor A for an appointment. Sure enough, when I met with him, the stakes rose.

> **Missions remained a scary, overwhelming proposition. How serious was I? More importantly (and more terrifying), how serious was God?**

Unlike his usual welcome, Pastor's eyes narrowed as I broached my subject. He interrogated me like a lawyer, contesting my thinking, fishing for false constructs. Where might I be romanticizing? Misled? Ignorant? I had no biblical training or background in missions. And although I worked with international women and student ministries, I'd never left the country. Was I willing to invest ten years before I was functional overseas?

I squirmed in the docket. *Does he think I don't have a call? Is this a red light?*

"You may be confusing evangelism with missions," he mused, citing the people I'd invited to church who ended up asking for baptism. "Not all evangelists look like Billy Graham. One way you discern a call is by its persistence. If this feeling persists, come back and see me."

As I rose to leave, he added, "One more thing. Tonight, ask God for clarity, and jot down your first thought on waking."

Our conversation wasn't exactly a green light, but I could live with a yellow one. The role of evangelist was more exciting than missionary, or so I thought after the Billy Graham Crusade. That night, I followed Pastor A's advice and asked God for clarity as I fell asleep. Was he calling me to missions or evangelism?

When I woke the next morning, words looped in my sleepy head: "Do the work of an evangelist" (2 Timothy 4:5). I sat upright, head rapidly clearing. *Now that felt like a call.* I also felt relief—maybe I could avoid becoming a missionary and having to eat eyeballs.

I spent the next few days scouring Scripture on an evangelist's work. When I told Pastor A about my waking word, he grinned, gave me two thumbs up, and suggested we talk again. Over the next year, Pastor A remained a wise, accessible, and realistic guide as we discerned together if I was called to missions.

But God wasn't finished. A short time later, he sent another missionary couple to present their work at Calvary—in a country I never expected.

France?

Harley and Betty Smith presented their ministry in France with Greater Europe Mission (GEM). At this point, my knowledge of missionaries was limited to Uncle Leo, the Barneys, Africa, and the biographies I read. Jungles were usually involved and those nasty diets. I didn't expect sophisticated Western cultures, especially Catholic ones. Yet here was an older couple, plainly dressed, talking about France.

Why France of all places? I wondered, skeptical. *Why would my church donations support missions in France and not somewhere more needy?*

As if reading my mind, the Smiths replied to my questions in the next part of their presentation. Most French called themselves atheists. In a country that embraced secular humanism, the Catholic Church remained an historical relic. Even the pope declared France a mission field. With my Catholic background, I felt convicted of my ignorance.

The Smiths presented their ministry in church planting, evangelism, and camp ministry. I knew nothing about church planting, and to me, evangelism meant Billy Graham. Camp ministry sounded solid, necessary, and effective, but not for me. My mind drifted back to my high school French class, with visions of verb conjugation and castles with moats. Maybe some French still rattled around in my brain and could be useful.

I studied the Smiths' demeanor as they spoke—guarded and wary, in stark contrast with Uncle Leo's twinkling eyes and the Barneys' joy. What were they not saying? They mentioned the oppression in France—a palpable presence. I'd never experienced the darkness they alluded to—or did I? I could think of a few unusual encounters—one in particular.

Good Angels, Dark Angels

While still on Long Island, Donna and I often explored the college campuses around us, attending classes, concerts, or conferences. One night, we were crossing a local campus green after some event. As we were about to turn a building's corner, something stopped me—gently but palpably. Pulling back a step or two, I stopped and studied the space before me. Donna turned and looked at me.

"What's up?" she asked.

"I don't know," I replied, reaching my hand out in front of me. Nothing. I took another step, but a terrifying sense of impending danger spooked me. Something was wrong. Hearing voices in the distance, we peeked around the corner.

Across the green, four men emerged from the shadows into the floodlights. Dressed in white clothing and black hats, they staggered like drunks and swung baseball bats. We froze, recognizing the gear from a cult dystopian crime film. When they spotted us, they shouted, pointed, and advanced like hunters who had flushed their prey. We fled.

It's unlikely two short women could outrun four men, especially men under the influence of some substance. But we did. We ran for our car, jumped in, locked the doors, and peeled out with screeching tires.

When we were a safe distance away and caught our breath, Donna questioned me. Who were those guys? How did I sense the danger ahead? I called it intuition but realized the Holy Spirit had warned us of danger. The "something" I ran into might well have been an angel.

In any case, these and other incidents gave me a category to believe the Smiths and other missionaries who hinted at the darkness they encountered overseas. At the time, Donna and I couldn't explain the intangible, invisible realities of the spiritual world, even though we bumped into them now and then. Now we have words and categories. And in France, the Smiths were combatting these spiritual forces of darkness. They belonged to a generation of missionaries who moved to Europe after World War II to fight another enemy—the enemy of our souls.

Camp of the Peaks

I signed up for the Smiths' newsletters, studying each one as it arrived. The camp work intrigued me—Camp of the Peaks in the

Alps. But I was more of an urbanite beach bum than a mountain-eer. The single women leading Bible studies in Paris caught my eye. Although I wasn't much of a teacher, I was born for café evangelism.

On their next visit to the church, the Smiths presented a construction project at the camp and asked for volunteers. *I could go,* I thought immediately—absurd, considering my physical condition. Just as quickly, I heard a familiar voice in my spirit.

"Will you?"

Who, me? The Smiths' voices faded into the background as I sputtered internally. *I would if I could, but I can't—I don't have a call. Or finances. I barely have a job. What about my back?*

I remembered how the missionaries, nuns, and priests defined a call—a mystical transaction, short on details, but something you knew when you heard it. The apostle Paul discerned a call to Macedonia through a vision in the night (Acts 16:6–10). Mary received her call to become the Messiah's mother from an angel (Luke 1:30–31). Moses's call to speak to Pharaoh came through a burning bush and left Moses sputtering too (Exodus 3). I could relate to Moses.

I saw no angels or burning bushes. No lightning bolts flashed. *Maybe I'll have a dream tonight. Or maybe it's all in my head.* After all, the Smiths hadn't singled me out by name. But as the service ended, I sought them out. Without mentioning anything about a call, I asked for more information. Harley handed me a brochure and circled GEM's phone number.

CHAPTER 7

France via the Bahamas
1989–1990

*Then I heard the voice of the Lord saying, "Whom shall
I send? And who will go for us?" And I said,
"Here am I. Send me!"*
Isaiah 6:8

B ROCHURE IN HAND AND HEART IN MOUTH, I LOOKED
for Calvary's mission chairman, finding him sweeping a floor
in the kitchen. What did he think about me volunteering
at Camp of the Peaks? He stopped sweeping and looked at me,
eyebrows raised.

"The church will contribute some funds," he offered.

I wanted to respond, "Just kidding!" Instead, I blurted, "I think
I'd rather raise the funds myself."

What was I thinking? I hushed my inner self and added, "If I'm
bound for mission work, I'd better start learning how to raise support."

He nodded slowly and encouraged me to call if I needed anything.

"Thanks, I will." I waved and hurried out the door, wondering
what had come over me.

Back home, I grabbed pad and pencil, brainstorming fundraising ideas: car washes, bake sales, babysitting, chores. I crossed them
off, one by one. Maybe a second job? I could barely manage one.
Maybe prayer alone, following some missionaries' example? *I'm not
sure I have that much faith.* Nothing resonated, so I put paper and
pencil aside and waited for inspiration.

As I studied the brochure, my curiosity grew. The commitment was only for two weeks. I could use my vacation time, meet missionaries in their country, and learn how to support them. Why not go? With no clue about cross-cultural work, I called GEM to volunteer.

The Magic Carpet Ride

Still percolating ideas, I went to work Monday morning to a fun announcement. Advent staff would attend an upcoming design show in New York, courtesy of some of our vendors.

A few weeks later, we boarded a bus to the International Design Center—a ten-story, thousand-windowed structure in Queens. Roaming the floors and showrooms recalled my days with Dad and Paul, exploring Knoll's immense spaces and Manhattan's city streets. I stopped by Knoll and other showrooms, looking for Dad's latest designs (he was still consulting). The New York vibe invigorated me.

Sales reps introduced new products—lighting, flooring, textiles, furniture systems. We networked with vendors for design solutions. At each showroom's entrance, a receptionist solicited our business cards, overcoming our reluctance with raffles and designer swag. Although the cards were bait for their sales reps, we dutifully dropped them in the fishbowls.

Two weeks later, a sales rep called, congratulating me—I'd won five hundred square yards of carpet. I had no use for carpet, but my heart skipped a beat. Could this be God's provision?

"May I have the cash value instead?" I asked.

"Of course. Let's see—the total comes to just over $500"—the price of my flight to France. *Boom! I'm on my way!*

Conversations with Carl

By now, we had voted a man onto Advent Design's island of women. Carl Mundell fit in perfectly. Fresh out of college, with a strong work ethic and sullen expression, he chuckled at our jokes and never took offense. He rolled his eyes and stuck to his blueprints as we teased him mercilessly.

A second design event one evening in Hartford drew the staff downtown, including Carl. While we sipped and nibbled happy hour offerings, I asked Carl about his life goals. He unveiled an astounding vision of owning a town named for him—Mundell Mountain. When he asked me about my dreams, I hesitated. Christian mission wasn't exactly happy-hour conversation at a design event. What should I say? While I stalled, Carl pressed me. I took a deep breath and began, sharing my plans for France and my $500 prize winnings, which would pay for the flight. Carl's reaction astonished me as much as Mundell Mountain.

"I want to go with you."

"What?"

"I want to go with you."

"On a mission trip?"

"Yes."

"But I'm going to work with missionaries."

"So?"

"Do you know what missionaries are?" *Did he not understand?*

"Oh, please," he groaned. "I want to do something worthwhile with my vacation and meet real people, not just visit tourist sites."

"But—"

Carl huffed and walked off. "Just get me the info."

I swirled my wine glass, digesting his response. Carl wasn't a drinker, so I couldn't blame alcohol. And as far as I could remember, he hadn't identified himself as a believer. Was he serious? Could someone who wasn't a Christian participate in missions?

The next morning at work, when Carl came in, I broached the subject again.

"Listen, Carl, about our conversation last night, were you serious? If you were just talking or being polite—"

Carl cut me short. He understood perfectly well what he was committing to—could I please find out what we needed to do? As he stalked off to his cubicle, I sat down and shook my head.

Carl was quite a bit younger than me, a hard worker, and a loyal friend. I had no reason to doubt him. Neither of us had romantic inclinations, and I wasn't worried about any monkey business. But the question of appearances and appropriateness troubled me. After consulting with GEM and my Calvary mentors, I received unanimous approval to proceed. GEM sent Carl an application, we updated our passports, and booked vacation time. The wheels were in motion.

God in the Tropics

I thought I had sacrificed my vacation time to work at Camp of the Peaks, but I underestimated God. Before France, he arranged a free trip to the Caribbean. Donna came home from work one evening to announce she had won two tickets for a five-day trip to Freeport in the Bahamas. Did I want to go?

We laughed often that year over God's extravagant gifts and let him spoil us. As Jesus promised, "No one who has left home or brothers or sisters or mother or father or children or fields for me and the gospel will fail to receive a hundred times as much in this present age" (Mark 10:29–30).

I was hardly making such a sacrifice. But apparently God notices every sacrifice—even a vacation—and generously rewards it. Maybe not immediately, maybe not in kind, but inevitably, the rewards come in this life or the next: "good measure, pressed down, shaken together and running over, will be poured into your lap" (Luke 6:38). The sacrifices pale in comparison to the gifts given.

> **Maybe I expected to escape like Jonah as we flew off to a tropical island, but God didn't send a whale to swallow me. He used a British preacher instead.**

Before traveling to the Bahamas, I asked God for one insight into missionary life. Although I thought my work would be in evangelism, God hadn't specified where. What if he wanted me to be an evangelist in mission? The puzzle pieces were shaping into an international picture, but the question still felt overwhelming.

Maybe I expected to escape like Jonah as we flew off to a tropical island, but God didn't send a whale to swallow me. He used a British preacher instead.

Gotcha!

We were on our way to Freeport, Grand Bahama's second-largest city, unaware that it was a party destination. Our package included several scheduled parties, but after attending one, we didn't need another. We preferred the beach, downtown shopping, and tiki-hut cafés.

On Saturday, we asked the poker-faced lady at our motel's front desk for a church recommendation. She usually answered our questions in a monotone, barely making eye contact. Now, however, she dropped her pencil and sized us up.

"Church?" she drawled, as if we'd lost our mind.

We nodded. She slid off her stool like an exhausted mother and dug under the counter until she found a chunky telephone directory. Leafing through its pages, she eyed us between scribbles on a notepad. We could be hooligans for all she knew, asking for the combination to the motel safe. Finally, she thumped the directory closed, pushed the paper over to us, and pointed to a phone on the wall. We called some numbers, chose a church, and asked her to arrange for a taxi, a request that provoked an eye roll.

Our journey to the church took us into the tropical brush, an hour from the coast and tourists. We entered a modest-sized church, crowded with whites and a few Bahamians. No one invited us to sit with them, so we took seats off to the side. To my disappointment, a white British missionary was a guest speaker that morning, and my radar went up. What was God up to now? I had hoped to hear a Bahamian pastor.

The missionary read Isaiah 6 as his sermon text: "I heard the voice of the Lord saying, 'Whom shall I send? And who will go for us?'"

I don't know how God orchestrates the lives of people around the world to draw them to an obscure place for an appointed hour to divulge his secrets. That morning, he chose a British man in a Bahamian church to speak to this American, delivering my next lesson in call. The convergence shredded any excuse I entertained about a call to missions.

In one of the great "gotcha" moments of my life, God turned the tables on me. According to Isaiah, I didn't need a call for missions. I could volunteer.

With the preacher, I whispered the end of the verse, "Here am I. Send me."

God must have fun creating these elaborate scavenger hunts, then watching minds blow up and lives change. I love his hide-and-seek, peekaboo nature, tucking surprises in unlikely containers—a British preacher, a colleague, a carpet sales rep. No wonder he brought me to the Bahamas. I'm still laughing, thirty years later, at God's playful character.

For a soundtrack, cue the click of Uncle Leo's watch case. The unlikely container held an intimate moment of laughter and camaraderie with a warm and generous uncle—maybe my first "gotcha" from God. As an introduction to his surprises, it prepared me for intimate, playful moments with God's Spirit.

In my experience, God draws me into his will with meticulous planning, humor, creativity, and attention to detail. It feels random until I hear that resonant click in my spirit—the ring of truth. Knowing God is sovereign can be dry doctrine or a harsh reality. But experiencing his sovereignty as he fulfills his purposes often feels more like a treasure hunt. I imagine his glee when I find the treasure. These divine "Gotcha!" moments always leave me laughing.

As we left the Bahamas, I stared out the airplane window at the tropical blues and blinding white beaches below. It looked like paradise, yet dark undercurrents were apparent during our short stay—barred windows, concrete walls, and barbed wire rolled atop chain-link fences. It stung that Bahamians didn't care to engage with us. History and television informed their vision of Americans. We represented wealthy oppressors, frivolous party animals, people who didn't care to engage with the Bahamians. In our short stay, I wondered if we'd done anything to change that impression.

I longed for honest dialogue and authentic relationship, without which we'd misunderstand one another. But I couldn't expect locals to know about my life back home any more than I could expect to understand theirs. Even if I lived among them and spoke their language, misunderstandings would abound. As a missionary, I carried cultural baggage I didn't realize—baggage that represented a threat. Without relationship and connection, I'd simply be a stereotype, misunderstanding and misunderstood.

Jesus interrupted my reverie. "And you'll never know what I left to come to earth."

He was answering the prayer I'd prayed before the vacation. I needed no more information and could no longer stall on the next question. Inhaling deeply, I exhaled the prayer God had waited patiently to hear: "Lord, do you want me to be a missionary?"

A year later, I found myself on a team at a construction site in the French Alps, sanding doors.

CHAPTER 8

Camp of the Peaks
France, September 1990

Let's go somewhere else.
Mark 1:38 NASB

SEPTEMBER IS A FABULOUS TIME TO VISIT PARIS. THE summer crowds thin out and temps moderate. Rain is inevitable but brief—maybe only a drizzle, a mist, or a moody fog. As Carl and I arrived, a morning shower diffused the rising sun. The City of Lights gleamed a smoky golden yellow. Before continuing to the camp, we had a day to explore. We walked our legs off, dazzled, checking off items from our bucket lists. After climbing the Eiffel Tower and Montmartre's thigh-busting steps, we finished at Versailles's palace and gardens.

Waves of language and culture shock hit as we tried to order food or decipher public transportation. Curbside crêpe stands were abundant and kept our stomachs happy. And Carl proved a genius in guiding us through subway stations. Of Paris's six major train stations, he also decoded the schedule and station for our train to the camp, near Grenoble in Southeast France.

The next morning, we bought our tickets and departed on the high-speed bullet train for the several-hour ride. The train sped south with a quiet *whoosh*, and passengers spoke in hushed tones. Even the conductor asked for tickets in a whisper.

We sat with our thoughts in the agreeable hush, staring at the passing scenery, nodding on and off in jetlag. The Alps came into view, then Grenoble, and finally the train station. We disembarked and connected with our driver, who drove us an hour through mountain switchbacks to Camp des Cimes—Camp of the Peaks. When we tumbled out of the Peugeot, Carl and I looked at each other and grinned. We made it!

Sanding Fingertips

The director, an American missionary, gave us a quick tour of the grounds, introducing us to camp workers along the way. Formerly an alpine village, the camp's rustic origins were as evident as the upgrades. The warmth of stone and wood created a welcome atmosphere. Thoughtful touches of hospitality added to the coziness. In the main dining hall, a fire roared. Alpine flowers flopped in vases everywhere. On one end of the camp, a beautiful mural decorated one ruin.

After lunch, the director mercifully escorted us to our accommodations in a building known as the Grange. Jet lag was kicking in—my legs wobbled up the stairs to my room. I was grateful for a makeshift cot in a private room with a common bathroom outside my door. The first volunteers slept on straw in a barn without electricity or water.

In the morning, I woke to spectacular sunshine. Wrapping a blanket around me, I opened the French doors and stepped out onto the balcony, inhaling the pure, crisp air of the Alps. What a reward for shivering under a thin blanket all night, listening to critters in the walls and ceilings. But I wasn't complaining. The inconveniences were minor compared to discovering a new corner of God's kingdom.

Within hours, a second team arrived like a jolt of espresso. A dozen or so high-octane Southerners from Greenville, South Carolina, jumped out of the van, laughing and joking. When they spotted Carl and me, they bounded over and greeted us like long-lost friends. Some of them had already worked at the camp and knew it well. Others were newbies like us. Their commitment to come for a year, leaving home, jobs, and loved ones, impressed me.

We were a jumble of French, European, missionary, and volunteer, and we worked hard all day in the Alps' beauty. At each meal, the staff cooked us regional specialties, answered our questions, and taught us simple words and phrases. On breaks, we explored every nook and cranny of the camp.

The leaders told us incredible stories of the camp's origins. In 1967, Harley and Betty Smith and team envisioned a camp for French young people—a place of beauty, camaraderie, physical exercise, and spiritual nourishment. Their team bought the crumbling remnants of an old village and began the herculean work of restoring them. With volunteers from Europe and North America, they created Camp des Cimes. Then the team planned a new building in 1984 to meet the growing demand. Construction began as volunteers and funds poured in. Now Carl and I, with the South Carolina team, lent our muscles to the effort.

My assignment, along with some others, was to sand 120 doors. Not flat panel doors, mind you, but French doors, with those tiny glass panes—dozens of them. If ever there was a bonding activity, sanding doors might be it. Working on sawhorses on an unfinished flagstone terrace, we sanded to 1960s tunes blaring from a local radio station, laughing as we tried to "name that tune."

Within days, our fingertips burned painfully, and we joked about sanding them right off our fingers. Gloves no longer helped, so for relief, we plunged our hands into the icy waters of a mountain spring, collected in a nearby trough. At night we dreamed of doors and mullions and fingerprints disintegrating into sawdust.

Though my fingers burned, my back gave me no trouble. I thought it impossible to stand on a stone-cold deck all day, sanding doors, and sleep on a lumpy cot at night without pain or spasm. What happened?

Freaks and Friendships

In between bonding and singing 1960s hits, Connie and I talked nonstop on the Lido Deck, as we dubbed our outdoor workshop. In one conversation, Connie described a man she had met just before coming—"I think he might be the one." Honoring her commitment to the camp work for a year tested that relationship, but to her credit, Connie fulfilled it.

A few days into our adventure, Connie received a letter. She waved it to me from across the Lido Deck—"From Stan"—and withdrew to a far corner. I watched as Connie read, grinning from ear to ear. Looked like love to me! Stan flew over for Christmas that year to propose marriage. A year later, on December 21, Connie and Stan tied the knot in their candlelit church in Greenville.

Carl and I drove down for the festivities, reuniting with others from the camp and meeting more new people. As I entered missions, Connie and Stan Beasley—affectionately known as the Freaks—were among my first supporters. They remain supporters, friends, encouragers, and Francophiles.

Bob and Jane Caldwell, the South Carolina team leaders, lived with their team in a rustic lodge up the mountain. And by rustic, I mean critter-infested crumbling stones and sagging beams. Their goal was to restore the ruin into a boys' dorm. A great big bear of a man, Bob is a builder, doer, and includer. One evening he invited Carl and me up the mountain to see "the Dorm."

As we toured the lodge, we ended in Bill and Roz Cross's bedroom. Roz's artistic flair in decorating "crumbling rustic" charmed me. As I complimented her, an ominous creak behind us turned our heads—Bob was swinging from an overhead beam, eyes wide. Our jaws dropped, some edged toward the door, and we all shouted, "Let go, Bob! Let go!" Fortunately, the roof held, and Bob dropped to his feet. In the morning, he added the beam to his punch list.

On the weekend, Bill, Roz, Carl, and I spent our Saturday driving up a high mountain pass in the rain and fog. We passed adorable alpine villages, nearly had a head-on collision, and found our own little Shangri-La. Stopping to pick up lunch, we spread a blanket before a crystal blue lake, nestled between snowcapped mountains disappearing into the horizon, and sat in silence. Eventually we munched on chunks of bread and cheese and clusters of grapes, with wine and chocolate for dessert.

Pushing on, the Peugeot overheated, so we let it rest while we rode a cable car three thousand meters up to a glacier. From that otherworldly landscape, we cruised down the mountain at dusk, marveling at the fairy-tale villages twinkling like stars on the mountainside. The descent was all the sweeter in the company of new friends.

When I joined GEM and Bob became mission chairman at Mitchell Road Presbyterian Church, he nominated me for church support. I was thrilled to be accepted. Now I have the joy of finding Bob, Jane, and my campmates at every mission conference I attend. And no matter how packed the schedule, I insist on "Jane time."

When that time comes, Jane picks me up in her SUV, and we grab coffee or lunch. I share my stories, and Jane, an empathic listener, clutches my arm, chews her lip, or grabs my hand. Her sea-blue eyes light up with wonder or fill with tears. Words of wisdom spill out of her, mixed with prophetic prayers. As we separate, a twenty-dollar bill finds its way into my hand or pocket.

Jane's signature laugh and bone-crunching hug will ever be a treat. Bob's leadership, humor, and humanity continue as he retires from the missions committee and begins a new ministry, still swinging a hammer. Each member of the team became a friend, prayer partner, and donor as I entered missions. And each time I visit Greenville, I stay with the Beasleys and everyone "spoils me up good."

One Hundred Kilometers

Everyone gathered in the Grange's meeting room on Sunday morning—staff, missionaries, and volunteers. The kitchen crew brought food and drink while the rest of us set up tables and chairs. I couldn't wait to meet the French believers.

Two middle-aged women arrived first, smiling shyly. They greeted us awkwardly, not knowing any English. After *Bonjour, Je m'appel*, and *Ça va*, we were stumped. I ransacked my brain for more French until the service started. As we moved to our seats, I grabbed the camp director's elbow. "Is this all? Two people?"

"Yes," he responded. "I know of one believer who lives about fifty kilometers over there"—he pointed east—"and another believer fifty kilometers this way"—he motioned west. "But they don't always come."

Two believers in a hundred-kilometer radius. Harley and Betty Smith had described France's dismal spiritual landscape, but the reality shook me. As I pondered it, the Spirit whispered, "I could use you here."

God always startles me with his flagrant disregard of timing. My mind swung between the French service and the click in my spirit. The Spirit's invitation—a call?—sounded playful, as if to say, "It'll be fun!" Not a word I associated with missionary life, but I had to admit France had been fun so far. And the Barneys and Uncle Leo—they were fun. My mind raced as the pastor broke the bread.

"The body of Christ," he intoned, passing the bread.

My mind snapped back to attention. I took a morsel of bread and passed the basket. *Christ died for us. He promised persecution. Missions would have its ups and downs. But fun?*

"The blood of Christ." The pastor raised a cup of wine and passed it.

"Given for us," we responded and sipped. *Sacrifice of blood by one who lost his life yet spoke of fun. As dangerous as driving in rain and fog up a high mountain pass. As fun as illuminated alpine villages and freaks from South Carolina.*

I sat on my balcony that evening, shivering in the cool twilight. The French and the missionaries had disarmed me—real, ordinary folks, jokers, and pranksters. Sanding doors, swinging from beams, restoring ruins. As a single, I didn't think I'd last in the camp's isolation. But God could surely use me somewhere. How could I sit in my comfortable pew in Hartford knowing only two believers lived in a hundred-kilometer radius of the camp?

Now what? Sitting with God on the balcony, I let the night engulf me and stared at the stars. Whatever this dangerous, fun God had in mind, I wanted it.

Au Revoir and Elsewhere

Carl departed the following day, and we circled him for a send-off prayer. A week later, it was my turn, and the crew encircled me. I'd only known the team two weeks, but I bawled my eyes out. I didn't want to leave. While I hugged and thanked the women, the men tapped their watches. Then we were off, back down the mountain, west to Grenoble, where I'd take a train north to Paris.

In my remaining evening, I wandered the City of Lights, stopping for coffee in Montmartre. I loved this artistic city—charming and historic, crowded with tourists. *But could I live here?*

On the flight home, I mulled over my two weeks. I had volunteered but felt called. Maybe I was an evangelist in missions. The two weren't mutually exclusive. Call, invitation, or volunteer—what was I missing? Why was I hesitating? Did it matter? I couldn't solve the puzzle but would be home soon, back in my Bible study, and needed to review.

Pulling out my pocket Bible, I flipped open to Mark's Gospel. My eyes fell on the story of Jesus withdrawing to a remote place and telling his disciples, "Let's go somewhere else . . . this is why I came" (Mark 1:38 NASB).

The words detonated in my spirit. Jesus had spoken directly to me, again—inviting me like a beloved child to see the Father's world, his wonders. Like Dad brought Paul and me into his world of designer showrooms.

I sensed the Father scanning my heart, like the prodigal's father scanning the horizon for his son. I could accept or decline, but if I refused, I knew my life would be diminished.

Jesus wasn't dragging me or ordering me to obey. The Father wasn't issuing a command. He wanted my consent, not my elder-brother duty. The call was unmistakable—a click with a flashbulb.

I sensed the Father scanning my heart, like the prodigal's father scanning the horizon for his son. I could accept or decline, but if I refused, I knew my life would be diminished. God would move on with or without me in France. What would I miss? How could I refuse? Why would I want to? I wanted to be like those in "the tales that really mattered"[3]—in the movies or missionary bios I'd read.

I asked the Father to show me how to proceed, and he promised to do so through Psalm 25, where I had somehow landed after Mark's Gospel. This psalm—with superb comfort, guidance, and instruction—soothed my spirit and quieted my mind. I fell asleep and deplaned a few hours later in Hartford.

---

[3] J. R. R. Tolkien, *The Lord of the Rings* (Boston and New York: Houghton Mifflin Company, 1987), 696.

CHAPTER 9

Dangerous Fun

Hartford, CT, 1991–1993

*And everyone who has left houses or brothers or sisters or
father or mother or wife or children or fields for my sake
will receive a hundred times as much and will inherit
eternal life.*

Matthew 19:29

B ACK IN HARTFORD, GOD PICKED UP THE PACE. I WOKE
early Sunday for church, where my heart skipped a beat.
Harley and Betty Smith were presenting another project in
France. *Already, God? We're moving forward already?*

After the service, I approached the Smiths to tell them of my time
at Camp of the Peaks. In response, they handed me an application for
service, which I stuck in a drawer at home. *This is moving way too fast.*

But God didn't stop. Within weeks, he used an economic
slump to arrange layoffs at Advent Design, and I was among the
first to go. When I received my pink slip, I filed for unemployment
and pulled out the GEM application. I stared at it a moment and
sighed. *Resistance is futile. Time to cross the threshold.*

I contacted Pastor A for a meeting. Before I went to France,
he'd shown little enthusiasm for me entering missions. His reluctance concerned me—without his blessing, I'd feel uncomfortable
proceeding. If he didn't endorse me, would GEM accept me? But
by now I knew I was called. I hoped he would support the decision,
however reluctantly.

When we met, I told Pastor A about the camp, my flight conversation, the layoff, and the application with GEM. To my surprise, he looked me in the eye and responded with the words I'd waited to hear: "I have no doubt you're called." Whatever hesitations he may have had, he never voiced them again. From then on, Pastor A never wavered in his support. We prayed, I thanked him, and then I danced out the door. Once home, I mailed the application.

A Trip to Wheaton

The following spring, GEM invited me to their spring orientation in Wheaton, Illinois. This three-week round of interviews, workshops, and psychological exams was preliminary to acceptance. Twenty of us arrived at Wheaton College, near Chicago, excited and a bit stunned to find ourselves in the process of becoming missionaries. But we easily connected over our journeys and passions.

Our schedules filled from breakfast to bedtime. Breakfast could be a chance to interview another missionary, another candidate, or a staff member. Evenings we ate in staff homes or were free to decompress with games or movies. As the staff knew, lifetime friendships would form in the group, and ministries might follow.

Sessions began with worship, prayer, and a devotion. Workshops followed on culture shock, cultural intelligence, and biblical studies on mission. During our last week, we learned about building a financial support team. In between, we met individually with staff, veteran missionaries recruiting for their fields, and a clinical psychologist. On weekends we visited local churches. We swam in a fishbowl through it all as the staff assessed how we interacted with each other and processed the material.

I asked everyone about working in France with a physical disability and received assurances the French medical system was more than adequate. And it sometimes offered therapies not approved in the States. I took the risk that physical limitations would not disqualify me for ministry. God would use the weakness as he did with the apostle Paul. I would challenge pain, move through it, and trust God to strengthen me.

One afternoon between sessions, I walked around to unwind and discovered a Billy Graham Museum on the campus. I entered and spent an inspiring hour absorbing more history and talking with the staff. Some had known and worked with Billy Graham, who was closely associated with GEM. Meeting these people and hearing their incredible stories spurred me on.

I longed for the lifestyle they lived, even if it daunted the daylights out of me. Like many missionaries, I felt compelled but inadequate.

Walking among such people and spiritual history (GEM and Billy Graham) whet my appetite for more. I longed for the lifestyle they lived, even if it daunted the daylights out of me. Like many missionaries, I felt completely inadequate but compelled. The work was beyond human capacity, but how else could we see God move supernaturally? Why settle for anything less?

So as the orientation ended, I learned with joy that I'd passed all the tests and interviews. In June 1991, I graduated from fishbowl to missionary and joined GEM for a three-year term. Certificate in hand (with a staggering budget to raise), I waved goodbye to new friends and comrades as we climbed into airport shuttles. We parted with a closing "See you in Europe!"—hoping we'd all make it through the gauntlet of fundraising.

The Gauntlet

Raising financial support is a fabulous deterrent to anyone considering missions. It severely tests call, character, and faith. It can still unnerve me in a heartbeat, but quitting wasn't an option. Maybe volunteering was a way into missions, but without a confirming call, I would have found it easy to quit.

As a novice, I had no idea where to begin. Thankfully, GEM assigned me a coach. We talked regularly to track my progress, brainstorm, and pray. She sent me a list of New York and New England churches that had supported GEM or a GEM missionary, and I pulled out the phone book. Week by week, I contacted more than one thousand churches over the next two years—a marathon of persistence. Now I thanked God for how back pain had taught me to persevere. I gained an education on denominations and how mission programs worked in each one. I also gained priceless insights into God's character and my own.

But before beginning this daunting task, as I was unpacking from Wheaton, the phone rang. The husband of one of Advent Design's partners called to ask about my time at Wheaton and specifically about my budget. When I told him the numbers, he whistled and declared, "You'll never raise that. Put me down for a thousand dollars." *Whoa!*

I hung up the phone, elated. My first donor! *Oh yes, I would raise that money. If God was in this, it was inevitable.*

But finding finances wasn't my biggest challenge. Like most people, my greatest fear was public speaking. As a child, I vowed I'd never do anything that required me to do so. Yet here I was, about to embark on an extended public speaking schedule.

The first time I had to speak to a congregation, my nerves were so high I felt sick. To make matters worse, I heard some nasty business in the church right before speaking. Negative thoughts swarmed as I grappled with the news. Did I even want the support of such a congregation?

I prayed until I was introduced and as I walked to the pulpit. But when I turned to face the people, the Lord murmured, "Look at my bride. Isn't she beautiful?"

I looked and saw ordinary people staring up at me expectantly. I stared back through God's eyes. Our divine groom was lovestruck, rejoicing over his bride. I remembered Jesus's story of the enemy sowing weeds in the wheat (Matthew 13:24–25). Where were the weeds in this congregation? It didn't matter. Though God would deal with them in time, this morning he was unconcerned. From that moment, I determined to guard myself against speaking negatively about the church—any church. It wouldn't do much good to complain to the groom about his bride. He wasn't listening.

Spa Days and Fine China

The following Sunday, I'd be speaking to another congregation about the same size—two services and one Sunday School class in between. I thought I'd faint. Donna accompanied me for moral support and helped me set up between services—my roadie, as the pastor dubbed her. As I took another walk from pew to pulpit, I prayed. And when I turned to the congregation, another word came: "I am with you always" (Matthew 28:20)—even in obscure New England churches, presenting missions.

The pattern continued. God stayed close, reminding me of truths, strengthening me with a word, creating the miracles. He set guardrails in my mind to think biblically about giving and givers. It was another scavenger hunt to find donors and divine appointments. Anything could happen at any moment. Unfortunately, Satan does some of his best work in churches and ministries, and I had several unfortunate encounters. But as my awareness of his tactics grew, God taught me how to deal with them.

As I ran the gauntlet, God transformed fear to faith, doubt to hope, ignorance to confidence. I discovered how valuable my partners are in brainstorming, discerning new calls, and sharing resources. So many became friends, encouragers, intercessors. Inspired by their examples, I became a more generous person myself.

My stomach can still drop when I face a crowd, funds dry up, or my car dies. I gulp, take a deep breath, and recall God's truths and faithfulness. He has taught me it's not about the money but the relationships. As I ask people to invest in my ministry, he asks me to invest in people. Together, we experience joy and witness miracles.

Over the years, I've received fine china, haircuts, luggage, airline tickets, medical care, a microwave, toiletries, spa days, tires, and journals. In lean times, I tighten the belt, sell possessions, or take a temporary job. The Missionary Care Center in Atlanta kept me clothed for years. When I'm not biting my nails, I'm opening the mail, and a check falls out—from a complete stranger. Funds rarely arrive on my timeline but are always on time. And God's provision often leaves me laughing.

In one white-knuckle financial crunch, he reminded me, "Not having funds doesn't mean you quit." Years later, he added, "And having the funds doesn't mean you continue. You stay or go at my word."

Thirty years later, I'm still here, underfunded most of the time, miraculously funded routinely. Funds come through the least likely suspects, like a carpet vendor, an employer's skeptical husband, or a brother's car donation. Occasionally I receive a game-changing gift that fuels a year of ministry. More often, it's a widow's mite or a child's allowance.

But that first year, I wondered how to begin and thanked God I had unemployment benefits. Before they ended, I had time to organize myself for fundraising and find work. I juggled finances, schedule, and pain management for over two years and watched my support team grow. The gauntlet was grueling, but I made steady progress.

The Finish Line

By November 1993, I had raised 80 percent of funds but hit a wall and risked burnout. After consulting with GEM, we agreed I could stop working and start drawing a salary from my GEM account. The hope was year-end giving would push me over 100 percent. If it didn't, I'd have to delay departure. I took the risk to save my sanity and enjoy the holidays. We'd review the numbers by mid-December, and GEM would clear me to book a flight—or not.

Resigning immediately from temp work, I relaxed for exactly one weekend before thinking about transition. The task list was intimidating, not to mention the emotional whammy, and the Christmas frenzy had begun. On Monday, I plunged into the chaos.

Applying first for a visa, I then registered for language school. After arranging logistics with GEM France field leader Howard Moore, I researched flights and shipping companies. Packing decisions followed: what to take, what to leave, what to give away. Fortunately, Donna planned to stay in the apartment until I finished my three-year term, so I could leave some belongings until I returned.

The painful goodbyes began as I dismantled my Hartford life, extricating myself from family, friends, church, and activities. I said goodbye to the International Women's Circle and the international students. For many of these women, I was their first (maybe only) exposure to Christianity. I hated to leave the rich friendships and exchanges, but they would continue without me.

Since the Billy Graham Crusade, I had brought a steady stream of people to the church, including Donna, family, friends, coworkers, and international students. I'd carefully built relationships and trust over years—not easily transferable. But I had to trust God. If he was calling me to France, he'd provide for my pew-mates.

As painful as these goodbyes were, leaving family represented an unthinkable rupture. Breaking the news to my parents was the hardest. It took us a weekend to talk through the emotional shock-wave. My mother was uncharacteristically supportive, but my father frowned. He thought I was making a mistake.

Adrenalin mixed with grief as the calendar flipped forward. How could I get everything done? How could I leave my tribe as Jesus taught? And would the finances arrive on time?

The holidays were a welcome distraction. We adults avoided talking about my impending departure. But the little ones asked dozens of questions, faces scrunched in confusion. Where was France? What was a missionary? Would I forget about them? Like me with Uncle Leo, they didn't have categories for missions.

And then the roller coaster lurched to a halt—the finances faltered, delaying departure. I notified the language school, Howard Moore, and the church. The prayer team, now numbering well over 100, amped up the prayers.

In the delay, I finished packing, sold my car, and spent more time with family and friends. We all waited and prayed through the holidays, and then the roller coaster accelerated. By early January, I had my funds and booked a flight.

On January 20, 1994, three years after Wheaton and nine years after the accident, I boarded Continental Airlines to Paris. I would spend one year in language school, followed by two years in ministry. With assurances that the French medical system could handle my back issues, I hoped for the best. *Who knows?* I thought. *Maybe I'll find healing in France.*

CHAPTER 10

A Year at Les Cèdres

Massy, France, 1994

In their hearts humans plan their course, but the LORD establishes their steps.

Proverbs 16:9

FOG ENVELOPED ROISSY CHARLES DE GAULLE AIRPORT, north of Paris. As I deplaned, a bewildering wall of language slammed my ears, still plugged from the descent. My eyes stung from crying my way across the Atlantic, and my throat burned in a haze of cigarette smoke. *Does France not know about lung cancer?*

I pressed forward, holding a photo of Lesley Fickett, my contact person, and searching for a sign—*Point Rencontre* (Meeting Place). I'd already spoken with Lesley, a teammate and veteran of several years in France. She was also single, and her sensitive and caring heart flowed through the phone call. I looked forward to meeting her. As the crowd bulged forward, I scanned the mob until I heard my name.

"Pat!"—a tallish, smiling lady waved at me. Rescuing me from the crush of people, Lesley pulled me to the side and out a nearby door. As we exited the airport, the warmth startled me. *Wasn't expecting warm in January.*

Lesley guided me to her car, and I stumbled along in wonder— *Paris!* Even an airport is fascinating in a new country. Lesley inched her car into rush-hour traffic, passing colorful pots of pansies—a welcome contrast to Hartford's snow and ice. As we crawled onto

Paris's ring road, I glimpsed forsythia along the highway, another astonishment in January.

We drove south to the suburbs, where Lesley shared an apartment with Susan, another single veteran in France. Susan greeted us at the door and ushered us to the table, where a cheery bowl of clementines glowed like a sunrise—a new day, a new beginning. On a dreary gray day, Susan's simple lunch rejuvenated me.

Another single lady joined us, Kyle Hunter, who could have doubled for singer Amy Grant. We'd also spoken by phone. Kyle was a more recent arrival and would help me with language and cultural adjustments. Like me, Kyle had an artistic bent and loved travel. At GEM retreats and annual conferences, we were often roommates. Kyle, Lesley, and Susan were involved in women's Bible studies in Paris, which I'd likely join after language school.

I faded in and out of the conversation, trying to stay awake until Kyle offered to take me to my language school in nearby Massy. I couldn't wait to see Les Cèdres (The Cedars)—my new home for the next year.

Day 1

We pulled up to a church-like building surrounded by cedars. A stout young German man met us on the doorstep—another student. After a rapid volley of French with Kyle, he whisked away my luggage and disappeared down the entry hall.

We entered to find Mme. Audibert, the housekeeper, smiling and nodding as if I were a neighbor dropping by for coffee. Draping a set of linens over one arm, she led us to my room, chattering in French, occasionally switching to English to hold my attention. She opened the door and dropped the linens on the narrow bed. Handing me the key, she wished me, *"Bon courage."*

Kyle and I surveyed the sparse room. My luggage took up most of the floor space. From the cathedral ceiling, a lacy veil of cobwebs hung in one corner. Dark-brown drapes drooped over the windows, which I immediately opened—someone had the heat up too high.

"I'm sure you'll make the best of it," Kyle concluded, and I nodded. The radiator thumped under the open windows. Before leaving, Kyle jotted down her phone number and promised to check on me soon. I thanked her and turned to my suitcases. Where were my pajamas? I couldn't wait to crawl into bed.

A knock on the door interrupted my thoughts. Dana, another American, introduced herself and handed me a bar of dark chocolate, saying, "You'll need this." I liked her already. After offering to take me grocery shopping in the morning, Dana left me to tumble into bed. Day 1 in France ended—or was it Day 2?

Cultural Adaptation

In one challenging year, I learned language and culture in a Christian school designed to prepare missionaries to live in French-speaking environments. In this bubble, we were like-minded souls floundering together. Les Cèdres assigned senior students like Dana to help newcomers adapt to life at the school.

Dana, a nurse headed to West Africa, taught me the house rules, including the unspoken ones.

More importantly, she brought me to the French supermarket and led me directly to the chocolate aisle. Dumbfounded, I stared down the aisle of goodness and back at Dana. She winked.

"The French say we need it for the magnesium."

"Works for me." I laughed, loading my basket with samples from several European countries. I never met a chocolate I didn't like.

Dana cautioned me against buying too much: we were allotted only half a shelf in the compact community fridge. We also shared cupboards—one shelf per person—and never mind the cockroaches. During the week, Dana invited me to her dinner group. I met several single women, most of whom were nurses headed to Africa. The group adopted me, and our weekly dinners became a welcome oasis on our journey through language, culture, and Les Cèdres.

On bad days, we commiserated and passed the chocolate. On good days, we clinked our wine glasses and celebrated. In a sea of change, our lifeboat of friendship bobbed with laughter, prayers, and tears. Having left home, cultures, family, and friends, we understood one another and the waves of grief, homesickness, and culture shock. Without these friends, I'm not sure how I would have survived.

Our simple dorms lined common areas, and a breezeway led to the classrooms, kitchen, and dining area. Though the dorms offered instant community, they lacked privacy. We were sixty in number, sharing paper-thin walls and unisex bathrooms. Even in the showers, we couldn't easily avoid one another, and we heard every argument. The constant need to communicate in a foreign language exhausted us.

We bonded over our bloopers, pronunciation labs, and the terror of public speaking assignments. Classes ran five days a week, with two hours of homework a night. We sat on hard wooden chairs most of the day and slept on well-worn beds at night.

Language wasn't confined to the classroom, of course. Whenever we turned the television on or left the school, we had to function in French. At the bank, cafés, and post office, we read signs, studied menus, and bought stamps. At the supermarket, we studied food labels to ensure we bought flour, not sugar, and yogurt, not shrimp (true story).

My salvation was a nearby park, usually deserted. After classes, I stretched my back and shook off mental fatigue with a brisk walk. Except for the occasional *Bonjour*, I didn't have to talk to anyone. I walked until dinnertime, braced for more conversation, and after dinner, disappeared to my room for homework.

Our rewards were the local French bakeries where we ruined our waistlines. On weekends, I went into Paris as often as I could, visiting museums, art galleries, and gardens. Usually I took the train with a buddy or two. If not, I traveled alone, unwilling to miss a chance to explore the City of Lights. I wanted to be with the French, listen to them, and steep myself in their culture.

Without a car, I walked everywhere—great exercise but problematic carrying bags and water bottles home from the supermarket.

As my back started complaining, I looked for the town pool, but its schedule conflicted with my classes. I muddled on—conjugating verbs in my sleep.

Word by Word

Before Google Translate, we strained to follow conversations, movies, and sermons. If we had medical appointments, we needed a translator. Add nonverbal communication, idioms, and cultural references, and we were soon lost and exhausted. Though we understood far more than we could speak initially, it took courage to enter a conversation. We blundered in with jarring accents and fractured syntax, struggling for words. I was grateful for the environment of Les Cèdres to practice constant humiliation.

The school had rules for its students: no visitors from home, no travel outside France. The goal was immersion to speed language acquisition. But the emotional toll was high, and most students broke under it. In sheer fatigue, we often defaulted to our own languages outside the school or in the dorm.

The staff encouraged us to find churches and language helpers outside the school—key to hearing street French, accents, slang, and colloquialisms. I joined one buddy on Friday nights at the home of Gilbert and Josy Boucher, who quickly became dear friends.

Each Friday evening, the Bouchers welcomed us like family, serving us drinks and pastries. With twinkling eyes and encouraging smiles, they talked slowly and listened patiently as we massacred their language. My friendship with the Bouchers endured until Gilbert passed in 2020. Josy survives him but remains in assisted living with health challenges.

While we crammed our brains full of words and phrases, I stuffed journals with impressions, emotions, images, cartoons, observations, questions, and sanity-saving verses. Sometimes I wrote in French and pasted in French hymns from my Sunday bulletin. Music aided memory and pronunciation. In the back of each journal, I wrote poems—a childhood habit.

One of Les Cèdres' first goals was to teach us comprehension. Even if we couldn't respond, we could understand what was going on. We were under strict orders to speak only in French, not our mother tongues. No matter the circumstances, the rule was "Only French."

Le Feu

Our professors were vigilant—swift to intervene for infractions, even when a kitchen fire broke out. Those of us present erupted in our own languages, quickly switching to English as flames licked a pasta box.

"Turn off the gas!"

"Where's the fire extinguisher?"

"Watch out for the towels!"

As we fumbled with gas knobs and frantically cleared flammable objects, the headmaster's door slammed open with a bang. He sized up the situation and seized an opportunity.

"*En francais—s'il vous plait*!" he thundered.

"*Oui*," we sputtered, groping for words, "but . . . *mais* . . . the fire . . ."

"*En francais!*" he roared, ignoring the flames.

Paulo ran for a dictionary and returned flipping pages as flames shot up the wall.

"*Feu!*" he finally shouted.

"*Merci*." Our professor bowed, closing the door and leaving us to extinguish the *feu*.

As an example of a gifted teacher seizing a teachable moment when he saw one, this professor remains unmatched in my lifetime.

Le Bouteiller

During our summer break, I participated in an evangelistic outreach in Lorient, in the western region of Bretagne (Brittany). As I walked along the village's coastal quay, a palpable sensation of home overtook me, which wasn't homesickness. I looked around. Maybe the familiar sounds of gulls and waves explained it. Or the

Celtic music playing through open windows and doors. The sensation faded—a mystery that lingered until I returned to Les Cèdres, where a package from my father awaited me.

In a long letter, with attachments and photos from his genealogy research, Dad had traced our ancestry to Bretagne. Even our name (Butler) derived from the French word *bouteiller*—the royal wine steward.

"You were right to move to France," Dad concluded. "Our family originates from there."

Dad's letter was a father's belated blessing and a stunning revelation. As far as we knew, our roots were in Ireland, not France. God's Spirit had led me to an ancestral home, one we knew nothing about, and Dad found the connection. His letter confirmed the uncanny sense of home I felt in Brittany. I wondered if an ancestor had prayed for someone to return to France as they fled the Norman Conquest in 1066.

Years later, when Leanne Payne became a mentor, I read her story of a similar experience in her ancestral home. She called it a "seeing"—a perception of the "Unseen Real."[4] I still ponder this mystery. Deep calls to deep, the psalmist wrote.[5] God works through generations—up to a thousand—and our personal stories enter generational ones.[6]

I had stumbled into our family storyline a millennium later. Soon I would learn about generational sins, blessings, curses, and their role in affliction and healing.

> **God works through generations—up to a thousand—and our personal stories enter generational ones.**

---

[4] Leanne Payne, *The Healing Presence* (Grand Rapids: Baker Books, 1989–1995), 24–26.
[5] Psalm 42:7
[6] Exodus 20:6; Deuteronomy 7:9

Changing Lanes

We weren't far into the fall semester when my back rebelled with the worst pain of my life. A doctor diagnosed lumbago and prescribed an opioid drug, which triggered hallucinations. I stopped them immediately and settled for bed rest and hot packs. Although I missed several weeks of classes, I graduated at semester's end.

As the year ended, decision time came. What team should I join? Throughout the year I had talked with team members, studied team dynamics, and visited their locales. Once a month we met with the Paris and Lille teams for prayer and fellowship in a conference center in Ecouen, a northern suburb. In other locations, an annual retreat drew teams nationwide for a weekend.

Each gathering allowed me the opportunity to evaluate the teams. Drawn to Lille, a northern city on the Belgian border, I met with the two families who worked there in church planting—the Moores and the Pilches. They had targeted two of Lille's southern suburbs: Wattignies and Ronchin.

Howard and Caron Moore from Canada had three middle-school-age kids, Stephen, Allison, and Patty. The Moores' distinctive hair color—from chestnut red to strawberry blond to fiery copper, rare in France—was known throughout the metropole. Stephen was an excellent drummer for our church, and Allison and Patty felt like my little sisters.

Jon and Esther Pilch met and married at Camp of the Peaks. Esther grew up in France, the daughter of Northern Irish missionaries. With four boys and a lone daughter, who had my complete sympathy, their humble home reminded me of my family—tumultuous, with a dash of Irish.

Howard wore several hats: field leader, team leader, and pastor of our church plant. Jon was his right arm, an elder in the church, tireless in facilitating events and outreaches. They both taught English classes. Esther was mostly involved in herding her five rascals, as was Caron, although both women ministered at events, outreaches, and among their contacts.

As much as I loved Paris, I was curious to explore a different city and region with few Americans. Like Hartford, Lille was a smaller, more manageable city. So I decided to join the Moores and Pilches, who welcomed me like family and started scouting for apartments.

My year of language study was over. I was more than ready to leave school but would miss my dinner club, the Bouchers, and Les Cèdres' wonderful international community. The tsunami of culture shock was diminishing, even as I braced for another wave in Lille.

Day by day, we students dispersed according to train and plane schedules. Again I said goodbye to people I hadn't known long but had grown to love and admire. Many of us stayed in touch for years. Others disappeared into the world. Each one made an indelible mark in my heart that I carried with me as I boarded the train to Lille.

CHAPTER II

Bienvenue Chez Les Ch'tis

Lille, 1995–1996

*But you are to seek the place the LORD your God will
choose from among all your tribes to put his Name there
for his dwelling. To that place you must go.*

Deuteronomy 12:5

A FASCINATING CITY, LILLE WELCOMES NEWCOMERS
with poppies, coal slags, and clouds the size of battleships.
France's fourth-largest city sits at the crossroads of Brussels,
Paris, and London. With different ethnic groups, its diversity
reminded me of Hartford.

Unlike Parisians, the *Lillois* (as they're formally called) liked
Americans—they met so few. After Paris's chilly reception, Lille's
warmth took me by surprise. One of my first interactions was with
a young lady in a candy shop. When I asked her where to find the
public toilets, she noticed my accent and asked if I was British.

"Americaine," I replied, and she lit up. Scooping a handful of
wrapped candies into my hands, she welcomed me—*"Bienvenue à
Lille."* Her open-hearted welcome made my day, and her friendliness
was typical. If you want to fall in love with France, Lille's a great
place to start.

The easygoing *Lillois* earned the nickname *Ch'ti*—for their
distinctive slurring of words that created the northern accent. Lille
also had a *patois*—each village with its own version. Neither French
nor Flemish, the *patois* was a fusion of both and more. I rarely heard

it in the city, except from older people who enjoyed sprinkling it into conversation to confuse me.

I looked forward to exploring Lille and Flanders, the region that included northern France and southern Belgium. Scarred with World War I's trenches and graveyards, Flanders's history is sad and bloody. J. R. R. Tolkien imaginatively portrayed it in his classic trilogy, *Lord of the Rings*.

But first I'd need a car. Over the Christmas holidays, I'd rented an apartment in Wattignies, about six kilometers south of Lille. While waiting for the movers, I stayed with the Moores, who lived just down the road. Howard took me car shopping, and I gleefully drove off the lot in a white British Rover—literally on the road to becoming a fully functional foreigner.

Soon my earthly belongings arrived from storage, and I had the joy of moving into my first French apartment. For years I'd worked toward this moment, running the gauntlet from the Bahamas to Camp of the Peaks to Les Cèdres. Call discerned, funds raised, language school survived. I sat on my balcony at sunset and toasted the occasion. On the threshold of full-time ministry with no map, I'd start in the morning. I couldn't wait.

But I'd never lived alone. I wondered how welcoming my neighbors would be and how to make friends. As it happened, a goldmine sat just around the corner.

On the threshold of full-time ministry with no map, I'd start in the morning. I couldn't wait.

Centre Promesses

Each town in France has its *centre sociale* (social center), offering community services and meeting rooms. Wattignies had Centre Promesses, a five-minute walk from my apartment. When I asked the team for suggestions on finding a language helper, they suggested I try there.

I walked over the next day and met Sandrine, who would soon become a friend. Sandrine organized a network of people willing to offer one service in exchange for another. She believed everyone had something to offer and had a knack for identifying a person's gifts, skills, and talents. The network was extensive and popular, thanks to Sandrine.

The network crossed age, class, culture, and ethnicity. Under Sandrine's artful leadership, a collective sense of friendship, camaraderie, and solidarity formed as people exchanged ideas and services. For immigrants, foreigners, and displaced people who'd lost their culture and language, Centre Promesses was a lifeboat. By inviting them to contribute to the network, Sandrine elevated each person's dignity.

Sandrine suggested I exchange English conversation for French—a perfect solution to practice French and meet new people. She paired me with six people seeking English, including Francine, who offered French. As a bonus, Francine lived in the apartment building next to mine, and we soon became friends.

By entering the network, participants could attend any exchange (French cooking immediately went on my list). As with Les Cèdres, within weeks of arriving in a foreign land, I had instant community. I met dozens of French and international people in a kaleidoscope of interactions, meals, costumes, languages, and accents. In contrast to the International Women's Circle in Hartford, I was on the receiving end of cultural adaptation.

On my first Sunday in Wattignies, Howard introduced me to the church. The response was applause and a round of *bisous*—the French greeting, distributed liberally to everyone in any social gathering. My second Sunday introduced me to another group I didn't anticipate: the police.

Car Theft

Lille's strategic location lifted it from its war-torn, coal mining, poverty-stricken past but came with a price tag. With open borders in Europe, drug-running and human trafficking were rampant along the Brussels-Lille-Paris corridor. Between France and Belgium, billboards flaunted the sex trade. It didn't take long before the dark side found me. The day after I bought my car, it disappeared.

As I left my apartment building to drive to church, I stared at the empty space where I'd parked my Rover the night before. I scanned the line of cars again, thinking I had missed it. But the parking lot was small, and I felt smaller. Then the Spirit whispered, "I'll handle this." *Okay, Lord. I sure don't know how.*

In Hartford, I would have called the police. In Wattignies, I searched my mind for phrases I'd need, like "file a report" and "car theft," but thought better of it. I'd need a translator, but since all the translators I knew were in church, I started walking.

At the church, Jon met me at the door and asked, "Everything okay?" I quickly filled him in while the church sang the opening hymns. He took me immediately to the police station, right around the corner.

The police were indifferent. In a border town, running drugs with stolen cars was common. They would search, but if I didn't hear anything within a day or two, I should start car shopping. My Rover was probably over the border, abandoned and burned.

Shocked, I completed the paperwork, then Jon and I walked back to the church. We arrived as the service ended and shared the news. A few remained to pray with me and offer their sympathies.

As I walked home, I asked God where the car was and how he intended to handle this. He didn't answer immediately, but as I entered my apartment, the phone rang.

"Is everything okay?" Donna asked.

It wouldn't be the first time God alerted a prayer partner to call me in some calamity. Though I couldn't easily communicate with prayer partners in the days before Skype and Zoom, God could. And this is how he handled many crises in my first term—by activating prayer partners he wanted to include in the story.

With uncanny timing, Donna would call within hours of something that destabilized me. She would pray and mobilize Calvary for prayer. Those unusual phone calls bolstered our faith—tangible evidence of God in action. And I formed the instinct to turn first to prayer, not panic, and wait for Donna's phone call. In a foreign country, to know God's eye was on me was incredibly reassuring.

The following morning when I phoned the insurance company to report the theft, another shockwave hit. Although I was convinced that I had theft coverage, the agent informed me I didn't. Arguing in French wasn't my forte, but I acquired skills that morning. My limited language and strong accent betrayed me, and the agent remained adamant. I called Howard to intervene. He had no success either, and I had no means to replace the car. *Dear God, let the police find the Rover.*

The faith-stretching wait mercifully lasted only two days before the police called. They had found my car in a nearby parking lot, with minimal damage. I could pick it up anytime.

"*Ouf,*" I responded (French for "Whew"). "I'll be right over."

My steps were light as I walked, thanking God for "handling it." After retrieving the car, I phoned Howard, who passed the news to the church. Then I called Donna, who called Calvary. A few days later, she reported a fun story.

One of my prayer partners walked into the Wednesday evening prayer meeting as Pastor A announced that my car had been recovered.

"So that's why I had to pray for Pat," she remarked.

Asked to explain, she unpacked the story. Awakened in the middle of Sunday night, she asked God who needed prayer. At approximately the hour I was arguing with the insurance company, she heard my name and prayed. She didn't know why until she walked into the prayer meeting.

If I had only a story of recuperating a stolen car, it would be cause for celebration. But God writes such better stories. He activated a global network of intercessors, including one with insomnia, and extended the party. My crisis wasn't all about me.

Road Tests

My next priority was obtaining a French driver's license—my international one would expire soon. Although I was an experienced driver, I was adapting to signs, rotaries, and traffic signals (on the side, not overhead). And because of France's smaller scale, I misjudged space—bumping into curbs, guard rails, and (gently) other cars. I practiced till I could parallel park anywhere on a dime.

Language was the more significant hurdle. Each evening I walked to a nearby driving school to study the manuals, review videos, and memorize vocabulary. I tried mock video tests for months before I could consistently hit the lowest acceptable score. When I did, my instructor scheduled the written test. I scored a perfect ⁴⁰⁄₄₀ and easily passed the road test. Her jaw dropped, the *Ch'ti* cheered, and I became a poster child for my driving school.

Furniture presented another challenge. It wasn't in the budget, I hadn't shipped any over, and thrift stores, garage sales, and tag sales were nonexistent in France. While waiting for funds to come in, I rummaged through items left behind by retiring missionaries and borrowed plastic chairs from the church. When the exchange rate tilted in my favor, I bought a sofa and a bookcase. By the end of my two-year term, I had furnished the studio.

Entering the medical and dental system in France with its specialized vocabulary and my limited one proved a fearsome challenge. My first dental appointment was an hour of terror—most dentists didn't use anesthesia. I called Sandrine immediately afterward to find one who did. She connected me to an Austrian nurse who knew Lille's medical and dental community—another goldmine for which my teeth were extremely grateful.

Construction

Life developed a new rhythm. Each morning I looked up French words and memorized phrases I'd need for the day's tasks. Then I'd screw up my courage, leave the apartment, and fumble through the hours. Afternoons and evenings were primarily given to ministry: visits, classes, Bible studies, or youth group activities.

Weekly I attended two Bible studies, a prayer meeting, and two adult English classes I would soon help teach. On Tuesday afternoons we met as a team, and Wednesdays were my day off. Once a month, we rose at dawn and drove three hours to Ecouen for our monthly field meetings.

In neighboring Ronchin, where the Pilches lived, the team attempted a second church plant, an effort we abandoned midway through my term. But we continued to facilitate the English classes, and I worked with Jon in the youth group. Caron, Esther, and I hosted some women's Bible studies, but few women were available between work and childcare. As my language developed, I began visiting women at home. What was key to the French woman's heart? What was her spiritual life like? What needs could I meet, and how could I pray?

In time, I proposed to the team that we begin targeted prayer for the people we were trying to reach. The Billy Graham team taught me the prayer triplet model: three people pray regularly for ten people until they encounter Christ. In Hartford, Donna and I took the challenge with another Calvary friend and witnessed God's movements in the people on our list. I wanted to try it in Lille.

Caron volunteered first. We picked a time to pray and compiled our list. Although I assumed we'd pick up a third person, we never did. Our results were more ambiguous than in Hartford, and then God redirected us.

I spent every available hour studying language and culture, meeting people, building relationships, reaching out. I longed to understand the *Lillois* and communicate well with them. Curious about their history, customs, and local *patois*, I asked lots of questions and studied hand gestures, facial expressions, and body language. I was more than halfway through my term and could barely carry on a conversation.

An Alternate Route

Despite the move, my back behaved while I searched for a chiropractor, medical care, and the town pool. I hadn't abandoned healing but had no capacity to pursue it with God. Adapting to France consumed all my time, energy, and headspace. To process waves of culture shock, I poured my questions, confusion, and impressions into poems.

While I concentrated on surviving, I found the pool and resumed my weekly swim routine. I met once with an orthopedist, who told me nothing new but gave me a prescription for painkillers. Relying on the pool, standard medical care, and the tricks I'd picked up over the years, I trusted God for an eventual breakthrough.

But despite my best efforts, my spine worsened during my two-year term. As cultural adaptation eased and pain increased, my attention and prayers refocused on healing. As usual, God was ahead of me. While I navigated culture shock and transition, he orchestrated an alternate route through an unsavory neighborhood, one I'd normally avoid. Devils lived there.

CHAPTER 12

A World with Devils Filled
Lille, Dunkirk, Ecouen, 1995–1996

Though devils all the world should fill, all eager to devour us, we tremble not, we fear no ill, they shall not overpower us . . . one little word can fell him.[7]
—Martin Luther

THE AVERAGE FRENCH PERSON IDENTIFIES AS AN ATHE-ist, so I was surprised how often they spoke of evil spirits. If they believed in evil spirits, why not good ones? When I asked about this paradox, the usual responses were a chuckle and a shrug. As one friend reasoned, "Evil is more evident. Where is God?"

After three wars on French soil in the previous century, the French questioned God's existence and goodness. If he existed, why did he allow such evil? Why trust him? Most rejected Catholicism, replacing it with counterfeit spiritualities. Witchcraft, occult practices, secular humanism, New Age, and Eastern philosophies were rampant. The French knew their astrological signs better than the sign of the cross. But these were the questions and practices of agnostics more than true atheists.

Lille's history of poverty, incest, substance abuse, domestic violence, and sexual deviancy opened doors for the demonic. Most women I knew were on several medications for mood disorders, and

---

[7] Edited by Don Matzat, "How Martin Luther Dealt with the Devil," *Issues, Etc. Journal,* December 1996, Vol. 2, No. 2.

depression was as common as a cold. Immersed in this spiritual soup, I noticed strange behaviors—tics, twitches, postures, and eye movements I'd not seen before. Were these symptoms of the oppression, torment, and palpable evil Harley and Betty Smith described?

Bedeviled

All these influences entered the church, of course. As I prayed daily for wisdom and insight, God used one young lady to enlighten me. Elodie attended our Bible studies and caught my attention with one unusual behavior. Each week, she entered smiling and engaged in the pre-study banter and chitchat. But when the study started, Elodie yawned dramatically, then went blank and silent until we finished. With the closing prayer, she reverted to herself and reentered conversation.

This behavior baffled me. Each week, Elodie attended our two Bible studies and repeated this performance. As we began, she checked out with an exaggerated yawn and reengaged when we finished. My questions multiplied. Why would someone attend two Bible studies each week, only to disengage? What was behind Elodie's yawn? Most people considered it simple attention-getting. If it was, what needed attention?

When I finally asked Elodie, she evaded. I let it go but bided my time. If we hoped to build a church, we'd need to manage these issues wisely and respond to cries for help however they manifested.

Besides, I liked Elodie. She was clever, fun, and we hit it off well. I hoped we could be friends.

Spiritual Warfare 101

I invited Elodie to accompany me to a regional prayer meeting in Dunkirk. We drove an hour west of Lille, arriving at the facilitating church, and sat in the middle of about fifty women. Little did we know our seating choice would give us a ringside seat to a demonic eruption.

During the opening worship set, a woman sitting in front of us fell from her chair, shrieking as if in pain. Elodie and I jumped back. Others screamed and fled, overturning chairs as they ran. Those who remained cleared a circle around her. Several leaders ran to the woman's side and knelt beside her. As they tried to calm her, she clutched her hair, shrieking and thrashing on the floor.

If ever a scene appeared demonic, this was it—something right out of the Gospels. As the woman shrieked and writhed, I wondered about the leaders. They couldn't seem to control the situation. Did they know what they were dealing with? *Did I?* As one of them ran past me for help, I ran with her.

"Is this demonic?" I asked.

Flustered, she stopped in her tracks, took my arm, and led me back to the group huddled on the floor, surrounding the woman.

"Here," she said, pushing me forward. "You do it."

Speechless, I stared at the leaders looking up at me while the woman on the floor shrieked. *Do what? I'm the newbie! This never came up in training!* But everyone was obviously at a loss. I found myself saying, "Let's move her to the side of the room."

We helped the woman to her feet and over to a bench on the side. This action alone calmed her. Now moaning softly, she rocked beside me, still clutching her head. Two women stayed with us while everyone else kept their distance. Some milled about in confusion, and the worship band stopped playing. I wondered where Elodie was and how she was reacting. Scanning the crowd, I didn't see her but called across the room to the worship team.

"Keep playing! Everyone else—pray!"

When in doubt, act with authority, right? I had no idea what I was doing, but my words galvanized the women. The musicians burst into powerful worship—no doubt flushed with adrenalin. Some brave women reset the overturned chairs and rejoined the worship. They sang with the urgency of an army under fire, not sure who was winning. The woman beside me whimpered, not looking up, clothes askew, her dark hair a rumpled mess. *Time for divine inspiration, Lord.*

With no plan, I placed my hand on her knee and prayed for calm. The two ladies, one by her side and the other kneeling before her, prayed with me. I ordered whatever tormented her to leave, and the woman went limp and melted into tears. She came to herself, thank God, and I turned her over to her friends.

My leader friend then approached and introduced me to the pastor's wife. She informed us the elders had been counseling this woman, who hadn't yet abandoned certain behaviors, leaving doors open for demons to attack. Jesus's words came back to me—how he often charged those he delivered from evil spirits to change their behaviors or the spirits would return (Matthew 12:43–45; John 5:10–14).

Spiritual Warfare 101 concluded, and I mentally cataloged its lessons: Keep worshiping. Take control with the power and authority Jesus gave me as a disciple. Warn those I work with to turn from certain behaviors or risk torment.

I spotted Elodie shaking in a corner and eager to leave. We drove home mostly in silence but would later debrief the incident. When we did, we also talked about Elodie's difficulty in concentrating during Bible study.

Spiritual Warfare 102

As the months ticked by, Elodie and I enjoyed a budding friendship. I invited her to participate with me in a six-week summer outreach in the north Paris suburbs. We'd work with our teams there, French believers, and a North American team. With the church's approval and financial support, Elodie agreed to come for a week. We drove together to Ecouen—the conference center where the teams would base. With her cheerful personality, Elodie integrated well into the international team.

On outreaches, we were alert to enemy interference within our teams—physical ailments, accidents, family dramas, or inexplicable foul moods. Sometimes the government refused permissions we needed for venues. One routine tactic was a disrupting spirit, tying up the team internally as we tried to focus externally. Early in the week, my introduction to this tactic came as a teammate interrupted the training session I was leading. Could I come? Something was wrong with Chloé, a young French believer on the team.

I excused myself from the session and followed my teammate to a large bathroom. A dozen women crowded around Chloé, comforting her. Some left on my arrival. Again, no one knew what to do—including me. But God had another lesson for me.

Chloé sat in a chair, panting or laughing oddly. Had she fainted? Was she hyperventilating or manic? Another missionary briefed me on Chloé's history, which included asthma and countless broken bones. Usually, she had a cast or brace on some joint. This evening, a pair of crutches leaned in a corner. I studied her face—impassive, not pale or sweaty. When her eyes focused on me, Chloé snickered.

"Go back to your class. I'm fine."

"You don't look fine," I answered, observing her. If this was another lesson on demonics, I didn't want to miss a trick. "What's going on?"

Chloé stiffened awkwardly. *Was that a sneer?*

"What's going on, Chloé?" I repeated more firmly.

"Nothing, I'm fine. You can leave," she snapped.

"I'm not going anywhere," I snapped back. With that, Chloé's arms and feet contorted, and I sensed the presence of something malignant. The women panicked. A few more ran off. I felt no fear but commanded, "Stop it." I wasn't sure who I was talking to, but I was angry.

Chloé's eyes locked on mine, with a malevolence that repelled me. I wanted to avert my eyes but repeated, "Stop it right now." Chloé started hyperventilating.

> Chloé's eyes locked on mine, with a malevolence that repelled me.... When Jesus spoke a word, the demons fled. Why are things getting worse, Lord?

When Jesus spoke a word, the demons fled. *Why are things getting worse, Lord? What do I need to know?* Someone wet a washcloth. Water . . .

"If you don't stop," I warned, "I'll throw you in a cold shower." I pointed to the open stall in front of us. Disdain washed over her face, but Chloé sat up in the chair, and her breathing slowed.

Several tense minutes passed. As we stared each other down, I pointed again to the shower. Chloé glared but broke eye contact. *Thank God. Is the showdown over, Lord?*

One lady remained with me. We waited while Chloé collected herself, straightening her hair and looking for one shoe that had fallen off. She thought she would rejoin the Americans playing games in the next room.

"I don't think so," I said.

Chloé's face darkened again, but with a child's petulance more than a malignant presence. I remained on guard. Chloé could barely walk. We propped the crutches under her arms and spotted her as she lumbered up the curving staircase to her room. As soon as we tucked her into bed, Chloé boasted, "When you leave, I'm going downstairs."

"No, you're not," I shot back. "I'll be back to check on you. If you're not in this bed, we'll just have to repeat that last episode."

I sincerely hoped we weren't in for a long night and asked God for help. With a scowl, Chloé turned her back to me. When I checked on her an hour later, she was fast asleep.

They Shall Not Overpower Us

Spiritual Warfare 102 concluded, planting new lessons in my spirit: God is present and faithful in demonic manifestations. He reminds us of scriptural truths and inspires us with creative ideas, like cold showers. Demons can exert physical control over believers, but we can control demons. Some demons are wimps—they don't like cold showers! And I didn't know a Christian, including me, who knew how to handle them.

The Moores arrived a few days later, on their way to vacation in Canada. I asked Howard for advice on the situation with Chloé. I didn't expect much—we were Westerners, typically unfamiliar with the demonic. But Howard surprised me.

"I know Chloé," he nodded, "and that would explain a lot." He recommended two books: *The Bondage Breaker* and *Victory Over Darkness*, by Dr. Neil Anderson, founder of Freedom in Christ Ministries.[8] He would loan me his copies.

We finished the outreach with no more outbursts from Chloé, although she and I kept an eye on each other. Other disruptions plagued us, which we took in stride. When we finished, I took an August vacation like the rest of France, reading the books Howard passed me. They didn't resonate, and books and study were limited. I needed hands-on experience, such as God was teaching me. Not that I wanted it, but more challenges were sure to come.

As my term would finish in a few months, I called Donna. Did she know anyone in Hartford who could mentor me in spiritual warfare and deliverance? My search for instruction would lead to the healing I had pursued for twelve years.

Transitions

When September arrived, France returned from *les grandes vacances*—summer vacation—and resumed its school-year rhythm. Students returned to school, workers returned to jobs, and we rebooted our ministry activities. The movement had a name: La Rentrée, and an event: Lille's world-famous *Braderie*—a citywide flea market.

As mussels returned to the market after the warm summer months, the *Braderie* also became a citywide block party. Picnic tables went up everywhere. Lille jammed with *Ch'ti* reuniting with friends to score deals and eat. The *Lillois* consumed *moules et frites*— Lille's signature dish—in massive quantities, washed down with

---

[8] See Freedom in Christ Ministries, www.ficm.org.

a Belgian blond. It was the last hurrah before we pivoted into La Rentrée and galloped through the school year.

For the team, each September was loaded with planning meetings to organize events and outreaches. We coordinated with our local and regional networks and renewed contact with friends and neighbors. I met Elodie again at the church and in Bible studies, still yawning. Otherwise, she was her jovial self and never mentioned the Dunkirk incident. I didn't know whether to pursue the conversation or wait—my term would end soon. Maybe it was best to talk after I returned, hopefully, better trained.

Perhaps Elodie sensed my ambivalence. She opened up one Sunday as we chatted at the church after everyone else had left. I took advantage of the privacy to ask her why she yawned at each Bible study. Elodie admitted that when she opened her Bible, her eyesight blurred, and the pages went blank. A ringing in her ears deafened her. Until the study ended, she couldn't see or hear. Speechless, I sat back in my chair. Where was the training for that? All I could offer Elodie was my desire to learn more and find help.

My three-year term ended a few months later, January 1997. Although I had completed my assignment, I considered it preliminary to a long-term one. In the States, I would debrief at GEM's headquarters in Colorado and reenlist.

I stored my car and belongings with friends and relinquished my studio, with its balcony overlooking the western fields. I'd enjoyed many a sunset there, with rainbows, hot air balloons, and battleship clouds. As a sanctuary, it had served me well. However, it was cramped. When I returned, I would upgrade to a one-bedroom.

To my church, students, and friends, I signaled my intention to return with the familiar northern expression *à la prochaine*—"till the next time." I departed with the satisfaction of a mission accomplished. Now came the reward—reuniting with family, friends, and church community. It would be a relief to operate again in English. I'd seek medical care and pursue mentoring in deliverance. What would the year bring?

CHAPTER 13

Intersections
Hartford, CT, 1997

*But if I drive out demons by the finger of God, then the
kingdom of God has come upon you.*
Luke 11:20

I MOVED BACK INTO MY OLD APARTMENT WITH DONNA, grateful for my own bed. In a lifestyle of transition, I appreciated familiar surroundings. When we returned from the airport, Donna pointed to the bookshelf, where two books awaited me: Francis MacNutt's *Healing* and *Deliverance from Evil Spirits*. Tucked into one of them was the name and number of a local pastor willing to mentor me in deliverance.

Like these two books, I considered healing and deliverance two different subjects, even though Jesus repeatedly connected them. I didn't understand how healing worked, and deliverance was completely foreign to me. As I leafed through *Healing*, anxious to start reading it, jetlag sabotaged me. I placed the book on my nightstand and fell asleep thanking God for new allies—and hope.

The next morning, I finished unpacking and caught up with Donna over breakfast. She worked as an independent consultant now, which meant a flexible schedule, and offered to drive me around until I found a car for the year.

It felt strange to reenter American life, adapting to its space and pace. For the past three years, missionaries, language students, and the *Ch'ti* had been my family. I missed them and the slower, more relational French lifestyle. But I looked forward to seeing my Calvary friends and community and to the family hooleys.

As we drove to Calvary on my first Sunday back, I noted how many churches we passed on one street. "Eighteen," I counted to Donna. "I think that's more than all of Lille."

We passed Mark Twain's house, Elizabeth Gardens, and the ethnic neighborhoods of the West End—welcome sights I greeted silently.

Throughout the year, I seesawed between remembering and forgetting. Remembering how to drive, forgetting traffic signals were overhead, not on the side. Remembering Dunkin' Donuts, forgetting how to pump gas. Remembering the cherry trees, forgetting banks were only open till 3:00 p.m. When I missed speaking French, I joined a French club through the International Women's Circle. Reentry would forever be living between two worlds.

Baby Steps

After settling in and seeing family, it was time to organize my year. My first priorities were finding an orthopedist and meeting with the local pastor for mentoring. I was already scheduled for a debrief at GEM's headquarters, coming up in weeks. For upcoming church visits, I'd need to order printing materials and create presentations. I started a list of calls I'd make to friends, donors, and churches.

In my call to the pastor, he readily agreed to meet me and recommended two resources. I knew both: Anderson's Freedom in Christ Ministries, which Howard had suggested, and Christian Healing Ministries, founded by Francis and Judith MacNutt. The same Francis MacNutt wrote *Healing,* sitting on my nightstand.[9] Both ministries planned conferences in New England in the coming months. I registered for both.

---

[9] Christian Healing Ministries, https://www.christianhealingmin.org/index.php?option=com_content&view=article&id=488:francis-macnutt.

While waiting for the conferences, I plunged into reading. Excitement rose as I read *Healing*. While the Anderson books eluded me, MacNutt wrote in a comfortable, conversational style. With thoughtful teaching and an almost clinical approach, he demystified the demonic and offered practical advice with biblical foundations. In straightforward language, he outlined a few key Scriptures so anyone could understand and continue Jesus's healing ministry. By the time I finished the book, I viewed healing through a new lens. MacNutt's work ignited hope in me.

Throughout the year, Donna and I read the same books, attended the same conferences, and discussed everything at length. As we read, we searched Scripture and applied all the inductive Bible study skills we'd learned at Calvary. We were on our way to an intersection that would change our lives.

Freedom in Christ

The Freedom in Christ conference came up first in Trumbull, Connecticut, hosted by a church that eventually partnered with me. My goal was to find practical tools for ministry in France. In no way did I imagine I needed the tools myself. I wasn't ensnared in the issues raised during the conference—spiritual counterfeits, trauma, sexual sin, eating disorders, occultism, and addictions. Or so I thought. But forgiveness, bitterness, pride—the subjects resonated, but I felt no conviction of sin. Either I was blind and deaf to God's Spirit, or he was biding his time.

In one session, Dr. Anderson took the whole group—over four hundred people—through his booklet, *Seven Steps to Freedom in Christ*.[10] With prayers, questions, insights, and affirmations, the steps examined seven areas of sin common to us all. The goal was three-fold: to familiarize ourselves with the material; to resolve any sin

---

[10] "Seven Steps to Freedom in Christ," Dr. Neil T. Anderson, available through http://www.freedominchrist.com/thestepstofreedominchrist.aspx.

we harbored before ministering to others; and to present ourselves as witnesses, not theorists, to those who came for prayer.

As we proceeded, the Spirit convicted me in Step 3: Bitterness vs. Forgiveness. He reminded me of a young man in France I needed to forgive. As Dr. Anderson led us in prayer and confession, I did so.

When we finished, Dr. Anderson asked us to close our eyes and observe our minds. What did we notice? I immediately noticed the utter stillness. In my mind's eye, I saw a vast lake stretch before me—smooth as glass, silent, and clear. Thoughts drifted in like distant clouds on the horizon.

Plenty of time, I thought, *to take every thought captive,* as the apostle Paul taught (2 Corinthians 10:5). The unattainable now felt possible. *If my thoughts formed this slowly, I could do it.*

I'd never enjoyed such mental clarity and wanted more. When the facilitators announced a *Seven Steps* training—leading others to freedom in Christ—I registered. The training involved three appointments. First, I would participate in two sessions as a prayer partner and observer, supporting the facilitator and the counselee. In the third session, a facilitator would lead me through the Seven Steps to experience the process personally. The first two sessions would build confidence and familiarity. The third session intended to expose any unresolved sin the enemy could exploit and build empathy for those seeking help.

I arranged dates for all three sessions. The following Monday, I was back at the church in a prayer room, observing my first session. A young woman sat knotting and unknotting her fingers, wrestling with suicidal thoughts, depression, and substance abuse. While a facilitator led the woman through the Seven Steps, I listened, prayed, and observed the woman transform before our eyes. Her pinched face relaxed after the first couple of steps, her eyes cleared several steps later, and she sat back in her chair as we finished.

"Incredible," she marveled, hands now relaxed in her lap. "I feel like a new person."

A door cracked open to a world I knew little about. Two things impressed me: how peacefully the session unfolded and how God spoke to me as well as the woman.

During my second observation session, also remarkably peaceful, God pinpointed my tendency to pride, rebellion, and despair. I jotted notes in my copy of the *Seven Steps,* squirming in my chair as I realized the French weren't the only ones who needed help. I, too, battled depression and abused painkillers. Although I'd never been suicidal, I'd consulted a psychic and practiced yoga—mentioned in Step 1. What doors had I opened to the dark side?

In my prayer times, I took myself through the questions, prayed, confessed, and affirmed everything God indicated. I was eager to move on to my third session but had another month to wait. God occupied me with a pop quiz at the pool one afternoon, handing me another piece of the healing and deliverance puzzle.

A Black Cloud

After an invigorating swim, I sang in the pool showers until I sensed the atmosphere shift. I looked around to see if someone had entered the room. A foreboding clouded my mind, stealing my sense of well-being. The clear lake in my mind was gone. Like so many gloomy days in France, I felt depression descend like a black cloud. *Oh no.* I panicked. *How is this possible?*

The Spirit stirred me to remember something from the conference: "Renounce the negative. Replace it with a scriptural truth. Say it out loud—three times if necessary." I acted immediately, anxious to dispel this darkness.

"I renounce this depression and announce"—what? In a split second, out popped, "The joy of the LORD will be my strength" (Nehemiah 8:10).

His kingdom had come, even to Hartford's YWCA showers.

The Holy Spirit rescued me, putting words in my mouth. All sense of gloom and doom vanished. The door God had cracked open in my training sessions swung wide, exposing what I perceived as a departing spirit.

So depression can be a spirit.[11] *And I can chase it.* More accurately, the finger of God drove it out, teaching me how, revealing the invisible world around me. His kingdom had come, even to Hartford's YWCA showers.

"They"

Three weeks later, I met with a couple at their church for my third session, the one in the hot seat. The pastor would take me through the Seven Steps while his wife observed and prayed. I arrived confident I'd check this last box, complete the training, and be released to facilitate the steps for others.

We chatted briefly, sharing our journeys into healing and the demonic. While I hoped the couple would have more skill, experience, and confidence than me, I was disappointed. Still, they were older, pastoring a church, and competent theologically. The degrees were on the wall. Although we'd never met before, they had also attended the Anderson conference, so we had common ground. In our weakness, God would enable us.

The pastor struck me as less confident than his wife, who answered my questions with the no-nonsense pragmatism of a staunch New Englander. *Good woman,* I thought. *Let's go.*

My first two training sessions had been calm, instructive, and enlightening. (I confess my expectations came from ghost stories, haunted houses, and *The Exorcist* film.) My individual session moved calmly enough through Step 1 but quickly took an unnerving turn.

---

[11] While I didn't know it then, I've learned depression has many causes, including spiritual. I would suffer another depression in France following a series of deep losses, which healed naturally without demonic complications.

Step 2 began with a doctrinal affirmation. We'd read it during the conference and debated if I should reread it. To be thorough, I did—or tried. Although I'd felt nothing more than the initial nerves, I suddenly and inexplicably broke down crying after a few sentences. Yet I had read it without difficulty during the conference.

Shocked and embarrassed, I apologized. The pastor and his wife sat motionless, waiting for me to continue. I tried again with the same result. With each attempt, I felt increasing resistance. *From where?* After repeated, embarrassing attempts, I admitted I was physically unable to read the affirmation. Sitting in a wing chair, I crossed my legs under me, feeling vulnerable. The couple prayed while I collected myself.

Finally, I forced the words out—with tears, confusion, and agitation. Baffled at my reaction, I accepted the tissues they offered. Wiping my eyes, I continued, reading and praying through the next steps without trouble.

With one final declaration and prayer to read, I was nearing the finish line when the opposition returned. I read the last sentence aloud: "I now command every enemy of the Lord Jesus to leave my presence." When I did, a voice in my head said, "We're not leaving."

I froze and reported this to the couple.[12] The pastor's wife stiffened like a mother defied.

"They must," she insisted.

"I know," I wailed, "but who are 'they'?"

Until now, except for my earlier difficulty, we'd prayed through the steps in a fairly clinical, rational way. Now we were grappling with something we barely understood. We were no longer ministry leaders preparing to help others. We were ordinary fumbling Christians battling enemy spirits. The demons were no longer in France, in a woman thrashing on the floor or disrupting an outreach. They were in my head.

---

[12] Our training taught us to report to the facilitator any thoughts opposing the Seven Steps process. In practice, I also began treating physical symptoms as opposition, as people routinely arrived for prayer with a headache or nausea.

I wanted to cry out to the couple, "Do something!" But they had no magic potions. This felt too much like France—leaders who didn't know what to do, and me, desperate for understanding. Novices as we were, had we opened a can of worms we couldn't contain? What happened if "they" didn't leave?

Once again to the rescue, Jesus delivered us. I sensed his presence beside me, steadying me and saying, "I'll handle this." The voices stopped, and peace and strength replaced fear.

I shared this, too, with the pastor and his wife. Before anything else could happen, we hastily concluded the session with prayer. But I left with no sense of resolution. At a nearby park, I sat on a bench to process the prayer session. *This story isn't over yet.*

A Visit to the Orthopedist

Next on the agenda was my appointment with an orthopedic surgeon. The visit delivered depressing news: herniated discs in my neck caused the severe pain and limited range of motion. I'd lost 40 percent of cervical function. When I reached 60 percent, the surgeon would fuse the vertebrae.

"I don't think so," I muttered to myself as I left. Yet how could I live with the debilitating pain and headaches? Was I missing something? Or still waiting on God?

Reactions from others remained unhelpful. I didn't need advice. I needed a word from God—nothing else would satisfy. Job, David, Paul, and the persistent widow had received responses—why couldn't I? Had I become like Elodie, ears blocked to his voice?

Sick of the guesswork, the veiled accusations, the problem-solving, I turned to God again. Convinced there was more to my story, I withdrew to my secret place with my new allies: Christian Healing Ministries, and Freedom in Christ Ministries. They offered hope. I read the ministry materials and examined the biblical stories. Twelve years after the car accident, I banged on God's door again for an answer. And God was about to deliver.

CHAPTER 14

A Panda Named Heal-Ling

Fishnet Conference, Vermont, July 1997

*I saw a woman bowed to the ground under the assault
of many whirlwinds. And I saw her regain her strength
pulling herself up, resisting the winds with great courage.*
—Hildegard of Bingen[13]

IN JULY, FRANCIS AND JUDITH MACNUTT WOULD SPEAK AT the Fishnet Conference in Vermont, which gathered New England believers annually for five days. This year, the theme was "The Father's Love"—nebulous enough to prompt me to call for details. In reply, I received vague answers. But by now, Donna and I had read *Healing* and were eager to hear more from Francis MacNutt, so off we drove to Vermont—the decision of our lives.

We weren't disappointed. The opening worship led by Ruth Fazal of Toronto ushered us into heaven in ways we'd never experienced. Ruth's mastery of the violin transported us. Some danced while she played. An artist set up an easel and painted near the worship band. For over an hour, we soaked in God's presence.

Then Francis MacNutt spoke, with an opening welcome to set the stage for the week. With a simple message, simply delivered, he reminded me of Billy Graham. The evening closed with prayer ministry, but Donna and I opted for an early night after a long day.

---

[13] Hildegard of Bingen and John Kirvan, *Let There Be Light* (Notre Dame: Ave Maria Press, 1997, 2020), 43.

As we snuck out, I spotted a pastor friend who led another church in Vermont that supported me. I waved to Debra and mouthed, "See you in the morning." She waved back and nodded.

Each day Ruth kicked off our morning worship, taking her time as we soaked in the Spirit. We migrated through worship, teaching sessions, and small group meetings, processing everything we heard. Over meals, Donna, Debra, and I swapped impressions. Evening worship recharged our batteries, and the days concluded with prayer ministry.

But that first day, confusing messages disturbed us. Some speakers had weak or questionable theology and teaching. The hippies were present, strolling barefoot in tie-dyed tee-shirts. Donna and I exchanged glances when an elegant, grandmotherly lady clutching a stuffed panda bear drifted before us in the crowd. Into what strange group had we fallen?

Again, we snuck out early in the evening as prayer ministry began, disheartened and growing skeptical about the conference. Maybe we were in the wrong place. Donna was ready to pack the car and leave, but I hesitated. After such high expectations and anticipation, I hated to abort our mission.

"Let's give it another day," I proposed. Donna reluctantly agreed.

Over breakfast the next morning, we shared our disappointments with Debra. She listened for a while before responding.

"You're here for a reason," she challenged us. "You're both mature enough to weed out the good from the bad. Why not stay and see what God has for you?"

Wisdom prevailed—we agreed to stay another day. If the teaching didn't improve, we'd leave. We cleared our plates and moved to the main hall for the first sessions.

Another sublime worship session rearranged our attitudes. Then the leaders rose for announcements, including their response to the previous day's controversial teachings. They had spoken with the speakers in question about the issues that disturbed Donna and me. Some clarified their teachings to everyone's satisfaction. Others had already left in disagreement.

Reassured by the leadership demonstrated, Donna and I relaxed and agreed to stay another day. Thank God we did.

As I listened to Dr. Mullen teach on the three-legged stool of healing—with physical, emotional, and spiritual legs—a light bulb went on. "Unless we address these three legs—physical, emotional, and spiritual—healing may not complete."

The Three-Legged Stool

Later in the afternoon, a new speaker arrived from Canada, Dr. Grant Mullen. A medical doctor with a mood disorder clinic near Toronto, Dr. Mullen presented a fresh, balanced, and biblical approach to healing and deliverance—with great humor. His clear testimony of faith in Jesus inspired us, and our excitement increased.

As I listened to Dr. Mullen teach on the three-legged stool of healing—with physical, emotional, and spiritual legs—a light bulb went on. I'd paraphrase his words this way:

> We start with the physical leg as the easiest to treat and do what we can medically for the patient. If we eliminate the physical component of sickness and the patient still suffers, we move to the emotional leg. We all carry emotional wounds, which sometimes cause physical symptoms—stomach complaints, headaches, back pain. If we heal the emotional wound, the physical symptoms may recede. If they don't, we examine the spiritual leg. How might the enemy be involved? Unless we address these three legs—physical, emotional, and spiritual—healing may not complete.

Boom. Here was a practitioner who categorized demonization as one leg of healing. Without this third leg, the stool would tip over. Connection made.

Dr. Mullen recommended Leanne Payne's writings, which had informed his lectures. After his session, Donna and I made a beeline for the bookstore. Payne's books had already sold out, but we could order them from an emerging online bookstore—Amazon. The books would shed light on the questions multiplying in my head. Although I had the tools for the demonic leg of healing from Freedom in Christ Ministries, I now had a holistic model, connecting the physical and emotional legs. Leanne Payne's materials would profoundly deepen my understanding of spiritual and emotional healing.

Now God set in motion what I'd sought for twelve years. Although I didn't realize it at the time, he'd been answering for years, giving me puzzle pieces to a bigger picture. This year he framed the puzzle, and the picture came into view. God built categories for me and equipped me with tools for ministry. And in the fullness of his timing, God passed me the final puzzle pieces.

A Game-Changing Question

Somewhere in the excitement of Dr. Mullen's teaching, it dawned on me: we were in a healing conference—why not ask for healing prayer?

I thought about it through dinner. Fishnet was a mixed spiritual bag (which included a wandering panda bear), but its heart was sound. Powerful worship and solid teaching continually ushered us into God's presence. A prayer formed in my heart as Ruth Fazal led evening worship. Whatever God intended for me, I wanted it. If counterfeits were operating, I trusted him to protect me. When the prayer lines formed, I looked for Dr. Mullen and stood on his line.

While waiting, I scanned the crowd around me. Donna was on one line, Debra on another. I focused on Ruth's worship and repeated my prayer, affirming my desire to receive God's gifts and nothing else. No monkey business. And then my turn came for prayer.

I explained briefly to Dr. Mullen about the car accident and the herniated discs in my neck. He responded with a game-changing question:

"Did you forgive the person responsible for the accident?"

The question stunned me. No one had asked it in twelve years, nor had it surfaced during my Seven Steps session. Memories flooded in of the accident. I couldn't remember anger, only shock. The man responsible certainly didn't intend the accident—in heavy city traffic, it only took a moment of inattention. *Had I forgiven the moonfaced man in black glasses?*

Dr. Mullen waited patiently. I focused on Ruth's violin, a lifeline in the riot of images tumbling through my mind. The day after the accident, the man called to apologize for my injuries. I assured him it could have happened to anyone. I'd probably be fine in a few days. When I hung up, I prayed it would be so and maybe included a forgiveness prayer. *Did I?*

Finally, I replied, "I think so."

"Let's make sure," the doctor suggested, taking my hands. He prayed a short prayer in tongues, of which I understood nothing. When he finished, I returned to my seat unchanged but convinced I'd received a key to my healing.

Six Years of Setting Suns

The following morning, for the first time in twelve years, I awoke pain free. Turning my head left and right in amazement, I told Donna. Hard to believe, an anomaly perhaps, I repeated neck motions throughout the day but never felt pain. I didn't dare hope—in case the pain returned. *Let's see what happens.*

What happened erupted later in the afternoon, after my small group. On my way to dinner, a memory—vision, revelation, or post-traumatic flashback?—detonated in my mind and viscerally in my body. I steadied myself against a wall. Images reeled of a phone call from my lawyer six years earlier informing me of my lawsuit settlement. He congratulated me on the amount, considering it excellent, but my heart sank. The payment only covered my medical debts. What about the future? A possible upcoming surgery? What if the disability worsened and I couldn't work? The lawyer cut me off, accusing me of greed. I slammed the receiver down, furious at his response.

My body tensed with anger as the images played. As they faded, I remembered a Scripture: "Do not let the sun go down while you are still angry" (Ephesians 4:26). And the Spirit asked another game-changing question: "What did you do with your anger?"

Six years of suns had set on that anger. How did I miss it? Shaken, I confessed sin I had never recognized—anger, an enemy foothold (Ephesians 4:27). With the Seven Steps prayers I knew, I confessed the anger, asked God's forgiveness, and forgave the lawyer. My spirit settled as I resolved this outstanding debt with God.

Why God chose a hallway for this encounter rather than my small group or a Seven Steps session, I don't know. But in that hallway, he finalized critical details on my healing—the spiritual leg of Dr. Mullen's three-legged stool. Once I confessed anger and forgave, the enemy no longer had a foothold. A few hours later, God would evict him and heal me.

Regaining my equilibrium, I headed to the dining hall and said nothing to anyone. My heart, mind, soul, and spirit were riveted on God. *Speak, Lord, for your servant is listening.*

An Acts 2:2 Moment

After dinner, as usual, Ruth Fazal opened the evening with worship. She introduced us to a song she'd just written—raw but complete.[14] After teaching us the chorus, she played the melody on keyboard and cued us on our part. Over four hundred people

---

[14] "Give Me Your Heart Lord," YouTube, https://youtu.be/Kw6IFJrZIMk; also available on Ruth Fazal's website: https://ruthfazal.com/product/inside-your-heart-cd/.

from different backgrounds and faith streams sang their hearts out. We had united through five days of worship, prayer, small groups, and meals. Many had received healings or breakthroughs. Others waited for theirs with rising faith. The conference ended in the morning—who would receive healing tonight? I hardly dared think about myself.

With one voice we sang:

> *Give me your heart, Lord, I want to feel*
> *Your love, Your love.*
> *Love undivided, love that is real,*
> *Give me your heart, O God.*

And heaven responded. A wave of God's presence swept through the room with a roar like a hurricane. I thought the pressure would rip the roof off. In confusion, people fell on their knees, crying out. A welling up of unknown tongues rose in the roar. Some clapped or laughed. In an Acts 2:2 moment, "a sound like the blowing of a violent wind came from heaven and filled the whole house where they were sitting."

I closed my eyes and prayed fervently. The commotion faded to the background, but the pressure of God's presence increased until I thought we would explode. It was a scene from an Indiana Jones movie. I kept my eyes closed, remembering "no one may see me and live" (Exodus 33:20). *He must withdraw, or we'll die.*

Trying to stand in the crushing weight of divine presence was maybe foolish, but I felt paralyzed. Then I sensed Jesus coming alongside me, one hand on my shoulder, the other on my back as if to heal. The intense, intimate gesture lasted only a moment.

The intensity receded, like a wave out to sea, leaving behind a jumble of people on the floor, kneeling or prostrate. Those still standing laughed or wept or both, praising God, clapping, dancing, lifting arms. A handful ran around the room shouting, some waving flags. I turned to Donna as she turned to me, tears streaming down our faces.

"I thought we were going to die," Donna said.

"Me too."

But we were alive, survivors of God's presence released in extraordinary measure. A buzz swept through the room as people burst into prayer, praise, testimony, and song. Some dear ones cried out, "I've been healed!"

A young man ran to the stage, pulling along the grandmother with her panda.

"Listen to this, folks," he shouted, grabbing the mic. Grandma stood at his side, smiling shyly.

"Who knows the panda's name?" he asked. A few giggled, and the crowd urged him on. He pulled Grandma forward. She leaned into the mic and whispered, "Heal-Ling!" And the crowd roared.

Well, why not? We couldn't stop laughing, overflowing with relief and joy. When Ruth launched into a song of celebration, we exploded with worship.

Whirlwinds

After a while, the leaders looked at each other, wondering what to do. We had one more session to go—but who could follow a visitation from God? The task fell to Judith MacNutt, who somehow managed an excellent talk on forgiveness with grace and humor. The prayer lines formed, but not in the typically peaceful and orderly transition. The crowd surged forward—the atmosphere electric with hope. I scrambled, searching for Dr. Mullen.

By God's grace, I found his line in the chaos and waited my turn. When he motioned me forward, I told Dr. Mullen of my day. Everything spilled out—waking with no pain, my hallway confession, and the sense during worship of Jesus laying hands on me to heal. I gave him more details about the accident and the other back injuries needing healing. Would he pray for me again?

Dr. Mullen took my hands in response and prayed in tongues. Immediately I doubled over as if I'd been gut-punched, though I felt no pain. Something wrenched me to the left—as if a whirlwind had caught me. I grabbed his arms, and he assured me: "I've got you."

Convulsive waves of emotion rocked me—ones I buried for years, but my body remembered. As if swept up into a tornado, I sensed splinters, fragments, objects swirling around me. I was reliving the accident—the crash, pain, trees, and stars swirling overhead. The doctor held tightly to my arms. Others came alongside to assist.

Another forceful twisting at the base of my spine wrenched me again. Like a snake uncoiling, a huge, malevolent presence emerged from my spine, enraged but impotent.[15] It dissolved, followed by two smaller spirits—grief and sorrow. I held on to the doctor.

Another movement originated at the base of my spine, firm but gentle, aligning my vertebrae. When the movement reached my neck, I collapsed on the floor. A man from my small group knelt beside me. While he prayed, Dr. Mullen and team moved on.

My mind whirred into overdrive—divinely recalibrating for a download. Scriptures on healing cascaded through my mind at lightning speed. As I watched in the spirit, God connected intricate pathways of body, mind, soul, and spirit, and how the demonic infiltrated. He synthesized everything I knew about healing and deliverance—and more.

When the download concluded, the Spirit had reconfigured my entire understanding of healing and deliverance. Jesus the carpenter had constructed my own three-legged stool and handed it to me. Though I was stunned witless, I knew two things with certainty: I'd just been healed and delivered of evil spirits.

---

[15] Some months after my healing, I read about yoga's kundalini spirit, symbolized as a serpent coiled at the spine's base. Yoga teaches postures and meditations to release this spirit. For some years before the accident, I practiced yoga for physical fitness, avoiding its spiritual aspects—apparently unsuccessfully.

CHAPTER 15

The Road Back

Vermont, Connecticut, New Hampshire, 1997

Have mercy on me, O God, according to your unfailing love; according to your great compassion blot out my transgressions. . . . Hide your face from my sins and blot out all my iniquity.

Psalm 51:1, 9

ENERGY COURSED THROUGH ME LIKE AN ELECTRIC current as I lay on the floor among a slew of people. In my ear, the Spirit whispered one Scripture (oddly enough in King James): "Woman, thou are loosed" (Luke 13:12 KJV). The words looped with another thought: *Twelve years I've lived with that thing.* And I'd just received the Spirit's equivalent of an advanced degree in healing. In a minute or an hour? I had no idea.

The man praying still knelt beside me, and when I was ready, he helped me to a chair. He stayed with me until I felt steady enough to walk. I thanked him and headed for Donna and Debra—wobbling like a drunk sailor. What would they think? But no one spoke. They, too, had received healings and sat speechless. Finally, we made our way back to the hotel, still lost in thought.

Regrouping

I woke at dawn, feeling something different. Jumping out of bed, I checked in the mirror.

"Donna," I called, waking her. "Look!"

Donna rolled over, one eye half-open. Turning at all angles before the mirror, I modeled my newly straightened spine. Pain from the "incurable" chronic fibromyalgia had also disappeared.[16]

Donna's eyes popped open, and she sat up with one word—"Wow."

We joined Debra for breakfast and chatted excitedly, comparing notes of the previous night. Although we tried to comprehend it all, who could? It would take months for my brain, emotions, theology, and psychology to catch up with my spirit. I wanted to thank Dr. Mullen personally, so I excused myself from the table to find him.

Dr. Mullen didn't blink as I explained my internal perceptions. His response floored me: "In my experience, spinal trauma is often healed when the patient forgives the person who caused the trauma."

The implications staggered me. I thought of all the people with such injuries and those who treated them. Dr. Mullen encouraged me to keep praying for my healing. In his practice, he rarely saw a spontaneous, complete healing. More likely a process had begun. I shrugged, thanked him, and agreed to pray.

As the conference ended, we said goodbye to Debra and other friends we had made. We lingered, reluctant to leave, still digesting this life-changing week. And we needed a game plan. Once we were home, how would we respond to anyone who asked, "How was the conference?" Who would believe us? I thanked God that in his wisdom, he had sent Donna and Debra with me to witness mind-bending events together.

Over lunch Donna and I decided to stay another day to calm down and brainstorm our

"In my experience, spinal trauma is often healed when the patient forgives the person who caused the trauma."

---

[16] A French medical doctor on our team considered chronic fibromyalgia a physical manifestation of depression.

responses. We hugged Debra goodbye and went to the movies. I don't know why we thought sitting through a film was a good idea. Shifting from transcendent miracles to Hollywood entertainment was impossible. Still feeling like I'd guzzled twenty cups of high-test coffee, I needed to move. We snuck out early and walked back to the hotel, where I went for a swim in the pool. After a few laps, I flipped over on my back and floated, praising God and reveling in my newfound strength and mobility.

After dinner we packed and set out early for our trek back to Hartford. We literally came down from the mountaintop as we descended through Vermont's Green Mountains. In six days, we had met God and received healing and deliverance. We were never the same.

Potholes

On the ride home, I marveled at the scenery and a pain-free trip. For twelve years, I'd never managed more than two hours in a car without having to stop for painful spasms. On this trip, well over six hours, we never had to pull over for me to stretch my back, only for food or a bathroom break. Back home, I slept like a baby.

But the following day, I woke to a painfully stiff neck and panicked. Was my worst fear coming true? I called Donna, and we grabbed MacNutt's book *Deliverance from Evil Spirits*. The next stage of my healing would literally be by the book.

Turning to the chapter on spirits associated with trauma, Donna read until one instruction: to ask Jesus "to go back to that moment in time . . . that continues to influence the person."[17] Following this advice, we asked Jesus to reveal anything we needed to know, starting with the accident. Immediately my mind flashed back to the emergency room—the brief but disturbing episode with the creepy man asking about my sex life. I'd completely forgotten the incident

---

[17] Francis MacNutt, *Deliverance from Evil Spirits: A Practical Manual* (Grand Rapids: Chosen Books, 1995), 189.

but now felt the anger it provoked. Once more, God asked: "What did you do with your anger?"

I had suppressed it, a pattern I'd need to investigate, but for now, I confessed the anger and forgave the man. As I did, heat flooded my neck. Anger turned to compassion as I realized he, too, probably needed healing of some trauma. I blessed the man, committing him to God's care. The pain vanished.

Relieved but speechless, my mind erupted with questions—*a forgotten incident twelve years ago . . . with a stranger . . . lasting maybe five minutes . . . creating pain? Why would God use pain to capture my attention? Is another demon involved?*

My brain swirled until the Spirit interrupted: "The incident remained a blot on your soul. You can't enter heaven with such a blot."

In the Spirit, I saw a chasm open between God and me—between his version of holiness and mine. *Who could cross such a gap? How could I resolve sins I'd forgotten? It wasn't humanly possible.*

"You're right," the Spirit responded. "But I'm committed to removing every blot so you can cross the gap."

Awestruck, I dropped to my knees, and the Spirit seared a name into my soul: *Jehovah-Mekoddishkem*—the Lord who makes you holy (Exodus 31:12–13). He set me apart as *Jehovah-Tsidkenu*—the Lord Our Righteous Savior (Jeremiah 23:6) and said, "I, even I, am he who

Could a forgotten incident twelve years ago with a stranger, lasting maybe five minutes, create pain?

blots out your transgressions, for my own sake, and remembers your sins no more" (Isaiah 43:25). Tears flowed at God's grace and mercy and his commitment to do what I couldn't: purge forgotten, ignored, or unrecognized sins.

God added another layer: I needed to forgive myself for feeling some responsibility for the accident. *If I'd been more alert and responded more quickly, I might have avoided it.* God exposed the thought as a lie. I was incapable of fully protecting myself.

This encounter rearranged my thinking. Now I knew the magnitude of the so-called "baby sins"—the white lie, unrestrained temper, office gossip, complaints. There's only one category of sin— ones that blot our souls and tarnish the *imago Dei* in us. I wanted no part of them.

Tormentors

For the next week, I woke each day with the prayer, "Anything else, Lord?" Morning by morning, God revealed issues related to the accident that I needed to confess or forgive. By the weekend, nothing came to mind when I prayed. To celebrate, I scrubbed the kitchen floor, an activity I'd rarely done in twelve years.

More layers of healing lay ahead, but fears hovered—fear of pain recurring, fear of anger. (Would I bury it again?) I feared more demonic deception, unnerved by the personal cost. Satan is such a stealth operator, his role hidden for years. Neither I nor anyone in my world suspected him in my injuries. Our ignorance allowed the enemy to exploit every foothold he'd gained over the years to keep me in bondage. Without the Spirit's revelation, I'd never have investigated demonic interference in my trauma. But as I identified these fears, I brought them to God for help and healing.

I had yet to discover God's power to keep me from sin and deception. But as I kept praying, worshiping, and reading Scripture, inviting him to speak to me, my trust deepened. By walking closely in step with the Spirit, my discernment grew. As the Spirit led, he turned the tables on the enemy, exploiting him to teach and trans- form me through a long and costly fight for healing.

And in his time, the Spirit bound Satan, declaring, "Thus far and no farther" (Job 38:11 TLB). He appointed a time, place, and person for my healing, affirming, "Should not this woman, a daugh- ter of Abraham, whom Satan has kept bound for eighteen long years, be set free?" (Luke 13:16).

Knowing God would clean up my "blots" instilled in me a sense of liberty to play in his kingdom and not fear mistakes, sins, or Satan. His Holy Spirit would warn me of temptations and convict me of sin. The Good Shepherd would guide me in right paths. Jesus promised, "You will know the truth, and the truth will set you free" (John 8:32).

I learned how elusive a forgiveness issue can be and how misunderstood the process. In my rush to forgive, I had skipped over essential emotional and spiritual work. Without a thorough process of forgiveness, the consequences can be severe. Jesus hands us over to the tormentors (Matthew 18:34 KJV).

"Torment" accurately described the cage of pain I'd lived in for twelve years. In managing physical, emotional, and financial issues with constant advice, recommendations, and accusations, I was ensnared in guilt, shame, anger, and resentment. Depression followed. There are no painkillers for spiritual sickness. But God untangles all the knots as we confess, repent, and forgive. Practicing these disciplines took perseverance, but the rewards were health and freedom. I became a maniac for divine collaboration.

Now if I hear someone describe such agony, I ask if they need to forgive anyone, including God or themselves. Almost invariably, the answer is yes. If they agree to forgive, we pray. Then, with one command, we can kick the tormentors out of their minds and over to Jesus. It's not quite that simple, but it's a good place to start.

I especially liked Lewis Smedes's book, *The Art of Forgiving.* I resolved to practice the art until I was slow to anger and quick to forgive—unoffended. Jessie Barney challenged me with Proverbs 12:16 and 19:11 and Ecclesiastes 7:21–22. I took those Scriptures to heart, aware of the chasm between where I was and where I wanted to be, and resolved to become unoffendable. It's quite a discipline but worth the effort.

Going Public

I was now halfway through my year in the States, and my GEM supervisor called to check on me. I gushed with happy headlines—I'd just been healed and delivered, and my support was fully pledged. After a few moments of silence, he replied, "That's the best report I've heard in a long time."

When Pastor A asked me about Fishnet, I shared my news, and he asked me to present my story to the church—in ten minutes or less. My first thought was, *Are you crazy?* How would I tell three hundred people a condensed version of an event I'd barely digested? How would they react? But crazy or not, I agreed, and we scheduled a Sunday in the fall.

When that Sunday came, I gathered my courage and bullet points and spoke for ten minutes. I received no negative pushback— little feedback at all. Like me, people had to digest the unfamiliar twists and turns of my healing. Pastor A was philosophical. The essential was done—I'd shared my testimony. How people responded was their responsibility.

And then a trickle started. Some came to me privately, asking for prayer or more details. Most needed to forgive someone. Word of mouth spread, and Donna and I prayed with perhaps twenty people. Almost all resolved a forgiveness issue, and some received physical healing or deliverance. Each situation was unique, and we learned from each one.

Shortly after, I participated in a mission conference at a New Hampshire church. I wondered if the church would receive my story. The people didn't know me as well as Calvary and were conservative, unaccustomed to healing except through medical means. But we'd enjoyed a warm and friendly relationship over several years. Did I have credibility? I asked God for wisdom and waited for guidance.

During the conference, I tried to read the crowd, hesitant to speak prematurely. But when the elders invited the missionaries to present a challenge to the congregation in the closing service, my heart leaped. Was this my opportunity?

I prayed that night and when I woke. If I focused on a challenge to forgive, it could work. I jotted down some notes, tucked them in my Bible, and left for morning services, asking God to lead.

When the evening service came, the pastor invited us missionaries to the platform. We had five minutes to present our challenges. When my turn came, I glanced at my notes with a quick prayer for favor. As I spoke, I felt great joy. Whatever the reaction, I had delivered good news.

A Sharp Curve

After the service, I drove to a motel near Boston on the way to my next stop. It was a miserable drive in a classic New England November downpour—the wind whipping and stripping trees bare. Leaves flew everywhere, adding to the slick conditions and clogging drains, creating minor flooding. With my windshield wipers on full speed, I could barely see in the pitch black. But I found my exit, slowed around a curve onto the street, and—*bang*. A car rear-ended me.

The shock was minor, but the spiritual implications shook me. Satan had just left a calling card. As I pulled to the side, a sinister hiss in my ear threatened, "Go ahead and talk. There will be consequences."

Maybe, I thought, not engaging the father of lies. In fact, I felt activated. Why would I stop talking? If I kept testifying, what did *he* fear? The Holy Spirit steeled me for the future. I prayed immediately to forgive the driver.

Although I felt fine, I guessed I'd received a minor whiplash. Fear gripped me at the thought. I pushed it aside and asked for healing.

A young man knocked on the window. Drenched in the rain, he crouched on the passenger side. I motioned him into the car. As he climbed in, I said, "I forgive you"—and told him why, in my top three bullet points. He nodded, wide-eyed and dripping. After exchanging information, we continued on our ways.

My car sustained no damage—*Thank you, Lord*. I drove slowly and carefully to my motel, arriving within minutes. As soon as I checked into my room, I fell to my knees. God and I had business to do. I was terrified, unsure of how much power Satan had in this situation. *Please keep me out of his cage,* I pleaded, till the still small voice whispered, "Trust me."

Within days, another legal process opened, followed by another medical exam. The diagnosis was "mild whiplash," which gave me little trouble. I healed within months.

I explained to the driver's lawyer my refusal to press charges or file a lawsuit. I even mailed him a copy of *The Art of Forgiveness*. *More consequences for Satan*, I calculated on my way to the post office.

My testimony had now gone out to the driver, two lawyers, two churches, and medical staff. Who was next? I'd soon be back in France. How would my story impact the French? How could I offer my treasured elixirs (as I now called them) to the community?

CHAPTER 16

Rue du Bol D'Air
Ronchin, France, 1998

*Lord, who has believed our message and to whom has the
arm of the Lord been revealed?*
John 12:38

WHENEVER I REENTERED FRANCE, MY ROUTINE
rarely varied. I'd head to the airport train station and
buy my ticket for Lille. Then I'd stop at the coffee shop
and order my French breakfast: pain au chocolate, those decadent,
square croissants chock-full of chocolate, and espresso. Sipping and
savoring the syrupy coffee and buttery chocolate goodness, I'd listen
as the French swirled around me. Soaking in the language, I thanked
God for the pleasure of hearing it again.

A crackling loudspeaker mirrored the French corner of my
brain—sputtering into life, searching memory banks, translating.
I listened for the *ch'ti patois* among the many accents and caught
new or unfamiliar words. Even in a year, a language evolves.

I usually had just enough time for my ritual before my train
whooshed in—the TGV from Paris to Brussels, with Lille in between.
Gathering my belongings, I'd make my way to the platform and
punch my ticket. Sometimes I'd grab a newspaper along the way.

The ride took me north out of Paris, past the graffiti and high-
rise apartments into France's breadbasket. Thanks to the constant
moisture of this humid climate, the fields glistened emerald green.
I always felt happy to be back.

The ride afforded me an hour transition before arriving in Lille. In the quiet, my mind drifted through the previous year's events and pondered the future. What would this next term bring? How were my language skills after a year off? What were my friends up to these days?

These simple rituals anchored me in a sea of cross-cultural transitions. No matter how wonderful the year home, it demanded stamina for an itinerant lifestyle and a surrender of privacy. ("It's not the years, it's the mileage," as Indiana Jones famously put it.) I don't know a missionary who isn't grateful for the first night home in their own bed after extended travel.

But this year, I didn't have a home. Until I found one, I'd stay with the Moores. As Canadians, the Moores understood transatlantic transitions. They made no demands and served beyond expectations. Their hospitality offered me elbow room to readjust to France while I looked for a new apartment. Though I had found my first apartment with miraculous ease, finding my second one proved a test for us all.

Rest Stop

As the coal slags appeared, pocking the green fields, I collected my baggage again. Arriving at the Lille train station, I disembarked and spotted Howard and Caron as I rode the escalator to the street. Their smiles, hugs, and *bisous* offset yesterday's tearful goodbyes. We were bursting with news and questions. How was the flight? How was the church? What's new in Lille? As we chatted on the drive to their house, my head swiveled in all directions, taking in changes.

While in the States, I'd given Howard and Caron a brief version of my healing over the phone, but we saved details till I returned and we'd have more time. For now, it was almost noon, when three kids would arrive home from school for lunch.

The table was set, and the kids already home as we pulled in. More joy exploded as I entered. Everyone started talking at once, in French and English. Their new pup, Brownie, greeted me at the door, leaping to lick her new best friend. As Howard muscled my luggage through the narrow entry hall into the dining area, we tumbled after him.

Lunch was another gabfest, with Brownie's head in my lap, testing her new friend for treats. Then the kids left for school, Howard for an appointment, and Brownie flopped in her bed for a nap. In the sudden vacuum, Caron and I looked at each other and laughed.

"*Ouf,*" she exhaled.

"I agree," I nodded. "And Brownie has the right idea—naptime."

Caron showed me to my bed and bath, giving me permission for a short nap. As she closed the bedroom door behind her, she cautioned, "But not too long." As we knew, better to power through jetlag than prolong the agony.

The next day, Howard and I retrieved my car at a friend's house south of Lille. The ride took an hour, enough time to share my story with him. I'm not sure Howard ever heard such a tale as I told that morning, but to his credit, he listened attentively. With only an occasional question for clarification, Howard never questioned my sanity, theology, or integrity. Driving back in our separate cars gave him another hour to absorb what I shared.

After lunch, Howard left for an appointment, giving Caron time to hear my story. As we cleared the table, I plunged in. When I finished, Caron took my hands—shaking from jetlag, fatigue, or nerves (I never knew how people would react). In the best possible response, she bowed her head and said, "Let's pray." Her instinct was powerfully healing in itself.

The nerves I felt evaporated as Caron worshiped God for what he had done. I owe an enormous debt to these dear friends who implicitly trusted me. They and the Pilches helped me resettle and lead us as a team into unchartered territory.

Lavender Carpets and Wallpaper

Now that I had my car, the apartment search began. Caron often accompanied me as I set out each morning on the hunt. When we returned home, we debriefed, brainstormed, and prayed. After lunch, I checked more listings and called friends and contacts for lunch and leads. Caron handled the domestic front, serving up our favorite French foods—quiche, crêpes, and *raclette*. After dinner, we watched films.

I asked for (and received) grace from the Moores as my stay prolonged. One after another, my applications were refused. I was single and a foreigner—a high risk for landlords. But finally a suitable one came on the market, and I jumped on it.

In Ronchin, between Lille and several international autoroutes, the location was ideal for ministry. I had easy access to Paris, Belgium, Germany, the Netherlands, and Luxembourg, with a bus stop outside my door. I'd be near the Pilches and the school where we taught English. And with minimal work needed in a country that left renovations to the renter, the apartment was a coveted find. I grabbed it.

Now I waited for the keys—another two weeks. Desperate for some divine intervention, I begged God to move mountains. He suggested I ask him for the keys instead. When I did, I received them within hours. We celebrated that night and prepared to move me the next day.

In the morning, Caron and I picked up some groceries and drove over to Ronchin. I pulled into my new garage—a luxury in a rainy land. Parking required an underground stunt of backing in several hundred feet, dropping Caron and groceries at the entry, then backing into a far corner. From there, we lugged groceries through a labyrinth of heavy doors, each requiring separate keys. The prize at the end was an elevator—thank God.

Riding to my fourth-floor apartment, I unlocked the front door with two more keys, and in we went—to a sea of lavender. My predecessor had replaced the carpet, a generous offer I gladly accepted. But I thought we'd agreed on a neutral.

And making matters worse, a seam ran through the middle of the main living area. I plopped the groceries on the floor in dismay. In response, a sheet of wallpaper flopped over on itself near the French doors.

With a sidelong glance at me, Caron offered, "It's not horrible."

"What goes with lavender? And that seam . . . I'll have to replace it."

"You'll think of something. You're creative."

"And the wallpaper," I groaned.

"At least the kitchen's in good shape," Caron countered. And she was right. To our astonishment, when my multicolored sofa arrived, it perfectly matched the lavender carpet—a divine sofa appointment. Over the years, I became friends with that lavender carpet—on my knees in transformational prayer times.

> I wanted to heal all of France, and here I was slopping wallpaper paste in a bucket for weeks. Or was God slowing me, stripping me of delusions?

A Breath of Fresh Air

Moving on from the lavender attack, Caron and I assessed the work ahead. We formed a game plan—making a list, taking measurements—and made countless trips to IKEA and Leroy Merlin (France's Home Depot). Once I had picked out fabric, Caron sewed drapes for the living room. Tackling the wallpaper project would be a challenge, and I knew just the person to call—Sandrine at Centre Promesses. She sent me a helper bee. For the next six months, I wallpapered and learned how to order hardware thingies in French.

The Bible advises us not to despise small beginnings (Zechariah 4:10), but I was beginning to despise this beginning. The readjustment period stretched out far longer than I expected and often frustrated me. Shouldn't I be more invested in ministry than wallpapering? I wanted to heal all of France, and here I was slopping wallpaper paste in a bucket for weeks. Or was God slowing me, stripping me of delusions?

As God asked me one day, "How long do you think restoration takes?" Excited as I was to heal France, I wasn't ready. God reigned me in with the wallpaper project, synchronizing me with himself, France, and myself. He had other aspects of healing to teach me. I slogged on.

In the slog, I considered the power of place to promote healing conversations. Although I needed a sanctuary myself, others needed one too. My little nest could be a shelter for all who entered—a place of healing.

Soon the gray main living area transformed into a sunny yellow to counter the gloomy winter months. The kitchen sported a warm Tuscan tan. Once I had a bit of order in those two rooms, I hosted friends and students for coffee, served on a wood plank over two sawhorses.

Under the kitchen window, I planted an herb garden on the balcony overlooking a linden tree in a quiet courtyard. The long, narrow balcony extended the apartment's length—wide enough to squeeze in a chaise longue and a small café table. I hung pots of geraniums everywhere and invited everyone I knew for a meal or *gouter*—afternoon coffee or tea, with cakes and biscuits.

This modest beginning was necessary to keep me in step with the Spirit. The renovations mirrored the renovations underway in me and my ministry.

Over the next eight years, I lived happily on Rue du Bol D'Air—"the street of fresh air"—with the linden tree, swallows, and magpies in the courtyard. The neighbors were typically private and invisible, friendly enough but expecting not to be disturbed. I hoped my presence in this apartment would bring a breath of fresh spiritual air.

Rebooting Ministry

As I resumed ministry with the church and English students, I absorbed the changes. A family of seven had left the church, leaving a sizable void in our tiny congregation and youth group. Elodie, who had secured a job, no longer attended because she worked weekends. And one elderly woman dropped out after a stroke confined her to home.

Unwilling to let Elodie disappear, I often stopped by her workplace after church to say hello and invite her for lunch or coffee. But Elodie's guard was up. She declined every invitation. It would be months before we renewed our friendship.

A new family had recently joined the church—Nadine and Jean-Paul, who suffered from so many afflictions they presented a ministry unto themselves. Nadine's two daughters, both married with children, rarely attended and related to each other like oil and water. The family's needs swamped our capacity. To cope, we worked with their medical team to set up a rotation of services to meet those needs.

By contrast with the pastoral work, teaching English was a relief. As I picked up classes again, I welcomed new and former students with drinks and cookies. We celebrated holidays—American or French—and they attended our Thanksgiving and Christmas outreaches. Each spring, the city of Ronchin sponsored a day trip to England for the classes—a highlight of our year. These relaxed times opened opportunities for spiritual conversations.

Over at Centre Promesses, the summer *fête* arrived to close the school year before *les grandes vacances*. Although I'd already lunched with Sandrine and a few others, I hurried over to reconnect with the wider network. Sandrine was making announcements on a platform as I entered. When she saw me, she shouted, *"Patricia!"* And with cheers and applause from the crowd, the *bisous* began.

"Now we know you love us," she added, blinking back tears.

Sandrine's poignant words pierced my heart, and I blinked away a few tears myself. I hadn't measured how the *Ch'ti* viewed me. It mystified them that I had come to Lille, and they didn't expect me to stay. Why Lille and not Paris, Nice, or Normandy—someplace prettier? Lille was a place to leave. When I did, they didn't expect me to return, regardless of my assurances to the contrary. In my second term, their guard dropped. The *Ch'ti* accepted me in new, deeper ways, and I had greater acceptance in cultivating relationships.

I noticed the same dynamic with my English students. Until now, although many grappled with serious difficulties in their private lives, they never confided in me, their "professor." It would breach a student/teacher cultural boundary. In my first term, when trouble came along, I offered a listening ear and prayer, which was always appreciated. In my second term, invitations came for a meal or *gouter*. People who knew me trusted me enough to engage spiritually. They were curious about my work and faith—a Protestant (as I was known) was rare in northern France.

With more acceptance, it was time to test the waters. How would the *Ch'ti* respond to my story?

The first friend I talked with listened quietly and said little. But a few days later, I received a thank-you card. She recognized a forgiveness issue in her own life and dealt with it. I would find that, as in the States, people responded more to the forgiveness challenge than to physical or demonic affliction. No doubt forgiveness was more accessible—healing was too much to hope for and deliverance too frightening to think about.

CHAPTER 17

Deep Waters and New Wine
Ronchin, France, 1998

Then they cried to the LORD *in their trouble, and he saved them from their distress. He sent out his word and healed them; he rescued them from the grave.*

Psalm 107:19–20

AS I SETTLED INTO RUE DU BOL D'AIR, THE SPIRIT TRIGgered the next phase of healing. I began a deep dive into Luke's Gospel, filled with stories of healing and deliverance, studying with new eyes, understanding, and assurance. When I read familiar verses that had cascaded through my mind on the floor at Fishnet, it felt like a reunion with old friends.

As a physician, Luke offered me another medical opinion of Jesus's compassion and healing ministry. One morning as I studied, the Word triggered another memory or vision from earliest childhood.

Scene One

My father walked in from work one day with an ecstatic announcement: he had bought a boat. My mother's joyful cry and their little jig in the kitchen signaled this was good news. I couldn't guess how, but Paul jumped and cheered next to them, so I did too.

On our first outing, the sparkling day felt like Christmas. Giddy with excitement, we hurried through clam shacks and lumberyards to the bay. A crusty old sailor sat on the dock, eyeing us. I thought he was a pirate. By the scowl on his face, he no doubt pegged us as newbies who would fall overboard, lose the engine, or otherwise create a ruckus. Without a word, he rowed us out to the moorings.

When we pulled alongside our boat, Dad jumped on board, helped us up, and the pirate rowed off. Dad hustled around the boat, tending to the engine, sails, and keel, while Mom fitted Paul and me with life jackets. Water slopped underfoot, rainbowed with gas dripping from the tanks.

Under engine power, we motored out into the bay. Dad beamed at the rudder, and Mom stood jauntily by the mast to pull lines at his word. Paul and I climbed up on the boat's sides, taking in the wonders of this new world. Then Dad gave the command, "Hoist the sails!"

No one warned Paul and me what sailboats do when sails go up. They catch the wind—and we caught a fierce gust. The boat lurched, catapulting Paul and me into the air as if on a giant Ferris wheel. Terrified, I looked at Paul, clutching the railing next to me. He was screaming, which meant we were about to die.

My father let out the sails, the boat righted itself, but Paul and I screamed on. Our parents tried to reassure us, but we were inconsolable, convinced we would die. To calm us, they lowered the sails and motored back to our mooring. Dad signaled the crusty old sailor, who rowed us to shore squinting in disapproval. We had confirmed his suspicions.

From that day forward, every weekend was a contest of wills between my mother and me. While Dad packed boating gear, Mom and I made sandwiches, and I begged her to stay

He exposed a fractured foundation in my relationship with Mom. It was an early psychological wound, a spiritual accident, a child's perception. My mother was certainly not out to kill me.

home. I hated sailing. I'd stay with my best friend. I'd do extra chores—anything but the boat. But Mom was adamant. I would learn to love sailing as she had.

My last stand was a meltdown at the car. While Mom ordered me in, I wailed and clung to the door frame like a cat on a screen door. Mom snapped (moms, you will understand) and screamed at me to get in the car. Something snapped in me too. I thought my mother was trying to kill me.

As this scene faded, the Spirit prompted, "Let's heal that rift with your mother. Do you know what snapped in you that day?"

I had no idea, but God knew precisely. "Trust. If you thought your mom was trying to kill you, how could you trust her?" He exposed a fractured foundation in my relationship with Mom. It was an early psychological wound, a spiritual accident, a child's perception. My mother was certainly not out to kill me.

Who has not experienced a similar situation—as parent, child, or both? Even a casual, offhand comment can be misunderstood and generate unforeseen fears and anxieties.

My early wound pales in comparison with others, but the relationship with my mother broke down. Our soul's enemy poured fear, lies, and suspicion into the wound, which led to depression and a spirit of death. As a child and into adulthood, I had no understanding of these dynamics. It was visceral. But now, God arrived to heal. With new insights, he led me in healing the breach and restoring my relationship with Mom.

Scene Two

I sat listlessly in the boat's cabin, waiting to die. The wind started whipping, and raindrops spit at the windows. I left the cabin, afraid it would flood. If I had to die, I'd go down on deck with the crew.

But on deck, chaos reigned. The lines flailed dangerously around us as Dad started the engine, shouting instructions to Mom, and pulling the wildly flapping sails down. A boiling black sky rumbled toward us, shooting lightning bolts into the bay. The storm was about to overtake us, and Dad strained to see in the wind and rain, coaxing speed from the engine.

Here it is. Death. Mustering all my childlike courage, I stood on deck to face it. I felt no fear, but Death was taking too long, and I grew bored. Sitting on the bench seat, I flipped a rogue line over the side, trailing it in the water. It snagged on something, jerking my arm.

"Dad, I caught a fish!" I shouted and started hauling. I pulled and pulled but couldn't manage it. *Where was Paul?* "Dad! I need help!"

You'd think in a boating emergency, with howling winds, flapping sails, thunder, and lightning, Dad would have ignored me. I'm surprised he didn't shout back, "Not now!" But he stopped, came over, hauled in my catch, and splashed it on the deck. Wrapped in blue cloth, the "fish" rolled against the other side with a muffled clunk—wood on wood. Curious, Dad unwrapped the cloth from a broken mast piece and spread it out. The wind quieted as if leaning over our shoulders for a peek.

"A nautical flag," Dad smiled, pleased. "The letter p—your initial." He handed me the line and continued saving our lives.

I stared at the flag and then up into the storm. Someone was trying to communicate with me. *Who?* In response, the wind roared, whipping the sails and lines again. I stood in the drenching rain, studying the rumbling black clouds. *Who are you?* Mom and Dad ignored me, occupied with the boat. I stood listening as Dad kept his eye on the shore and brought us in safely. We had cheated Death.

Did the one who sent me the flag save us? I fell asleep that night wondering. In the morning, I couldn't wait to go sailing. I'd look up to the sky and wait for another signal from the invisible someone who sent me the flag. Maybe he was best reached by boat.

Fifty years later, as the scene concluded, the invisible someone whispered, "That was me. I have called you by name, you are mine" (Isaiah 43:1)—my life verse.

New Wine

I shared these scenes with Caron the following Friday. Astonished as we were, we agreed to adjust our weekly prayer times to pursue these inner healings God was revealing. If he was pouring new wine, we needed a new wineskin. We were in France for the long haul and didn't want to be two more missionary casualties. The healthier we were, the longer we'd survive and the better we could serve others. In the safety and privacy of our Friday mornings, we committed to do the work.

Our ground rules were honesty and transparency, with no judgment, criticism, advice, or problem-solving unless requested. But we committed to challenge, affirm, and correct one another. As we met weekly, we shared insights, confessions, struggles, and temptations. We encouraged one another, held each other accountable, and celebrated victories. When one of us floundered, the other prayed.

If we veered into introspection, negativity, or overanalyzing, we checked ourselves. For some of the thornier challenges in church planting, we tested our perceptions and sought God for wisdom. It took years to dismantle our dysfunctional patterns. But as we acknowledged fears, offenses, insight, and sins, we gradually created healthier practices. As we matured in our thinking, our ministry matured.

These invaluable prayer times continued for years—a priceless gift of spiritual growth and stability. They anchored us to grow and thrive amid stiff challenges in France. Without our Friday mornings, I don't know how we would have sustained the pressures.

As spring passed into summer, we considered how to organize another ministry year at La Rentrée. I would continue with my English classes and the Centre Promesses network, building relationships. Caron and I planned a Bible study with the church women, and I scheduled one with a French friend. With our colleagues in Paris, we attended their annual Christian Women's Club retreat. Caron and I would look for ways to pursue healing ministry—both in practice and in building sound theology to tackle the questions and controversies surrounding the subject. Howard arranged for me to give a workshop at our upcoming annual retreat.

As my healing progressed, artistic and creative gifts emerged that I could no longer ignore, nor did I want to—they brought joy. If I neglected them, they nagged. But I had a block—Dad's advice in high school: "Keep the arts as a hobby but find a job that pays."

During meetings with my high school counselor to look at college choices, we had considered journalism. Having won honors and awards for English and writing through my school years, I assumed these would be my life's work. Instead, the counselor shocked me by recommending I now put writing aside. It was a strength, she agreed, but it wouldn't pay the bills.

Put aside writing? Pop went my bubble, my life's goal. The advice sent me into the world to look for other work, my "gift" consigned to journals.

My heavenly Father disagreed, however, and enlightened me one day in France: "It's not my idea to keep the gifts I give as hobbies. They're intended for the kingdom."

The Hero's Journey

To cultivate my writing skills, I signed up for an online course, which used *The Writer's Journey* as its textbook.[18] The book introduced me to the literary device known as the hero's journey, describing a typical adventure of the archetype known as the hero. As I read, my imagination ignited. The hero's journey accurately described the passage of a soul through life—more vividly than anything I'd heard in the church. Specifically, it illuminated my healing journey.

As I worked with the material, I plotted the events surrounding my healing within the hero's journey structure. Random events now connected and looked intentional—scripted with excellence by a

---

[18] Christopher Vogler, *The Writer's Journey, 2nd Ed.* (Studio City: Michael Wiese Productions, 1998).

master storyteller. I sat in awe of God's elegant design in leading me to healing. In hero's journey jargon, I had crossed thresholds and met allies, mentors, threshold guardians, and an archenemy. I seized my reward in a cave of doubt and brought elixirs like forgiveness back to my community.

I hadn't encountered anything like the hero's journey relating to spiritual life, connecting intellect and imagination. And I haven't stopped using it. A decade later, when asked to create a curriculum for artists, I pulled *The Writer's Journey* off the shelf and wrote for a year. For ten more years, I taught it, and a half-baked manuscript waits in the wings for my attention.

I wondered how to use the hero's journey in evangelism and discipleship. Most of my contacts were in the arts. Christian jargon didn't fly in a secular humanistic culture, least of all in the arts. Fresh language, a compelling metanarrative (God's story), archetypes— could the hero's journey translate spiritual life to those who were more conversant in film than Scripture?

Convinced the French would respond to demonstrations of God's power to heal, I also knew they loved a good story. While I incorporated the hero's journey into my writing and faith, I began framing spirituality in its language and metaphors. With the universal language of storytelling, I had a new vocabulary to satisfy the French mind and heart. People could readily relate to familiar films, scenes, and characters.

Archetypes—those characters typical and essential to a good story or film—became examples to cite in conversations. A YouTube clip could speak volumes to the heart, imaginatively illustrating biblical principles.[19] Building a theological framework took time. Explaining it through the hero's journey held everyone's attention.

Viewing a movie and discussing it over coffee proved more amenable to spiritual insight than an invitation to a Bible study.

---

[19] BibleProject has mastered the art of animated biblical storytelling; https://bibleproject.com/.

I could bypass the keen French intellect and disdain for religion with stories from *Star Wars* or *Lord of the Rings.* I watched eyes light up with understanding.

Story, as piercing and succinct as Jesus's parables, became an essential component of my work as a church planter and eventual pastoral care counselor. A Latin culture, France had passion as fierce as her intellect. We needed to engage both to reach the French heart, which would take imagination, revelation, demonstration. And story, film, and parable.

The hero's journey was my new tool to lower the barriers and engage the French. As La Rentrée approached, I asked God to increase my skill in writing and ministry through the hero's journey.

He started with a stranger named Yvonne.

CHAPTER 18

Cured or Healed?

Lille, France, 1998–1999

*For we're newcomers at this, with a lot to learn, and not
too long to learn it.*
Job 8:9 MSG

O
NE RAINY DAY I DROPPED IN TO SEE NADINE. WHEN
I knocked, she called out to enter. I poked my head in the
door with a robust "Bonjour!" and Nadine lit up—"Patricia!" As she rocked herself up from the couch, I stuck my umbrella
in a corner and waited till she stood and corrected for vertigo. Then
she grabbed my shoulders, and we exchanged *bisous*.

Nadine was attached to an IV drip and stand, a common
homecare practice in France. With a background of trauma and
abuse, she had complex medical issues. Yet somehow, Nadine kept
a childlike spirit. And with North African heritage, her door was
always open to guests, with a coffeepot warming on the stove.

Nadine waved me to the kitchen table while she fetched the
coffee, talking a blue streak. Directing me to pull mugs and biscuits
from an overhead cupboard, she poured the coffee, parked her IV
stand, and plunked herself at the table. I sat opposite her, setting
down cups and—after checking for roaches—an open packet of
biscuits. Nadine wiped a plate with her housecoat and emptied the
biscuits on it.

We'd barely settled when a neighbor burst in, rain rolling off
her broad shoulders and hair slicked back into a black mat. She was

shaking like a leaf and on the verge of tears. Unfazed, Nadine pulled out a chair and poured another cup of coffee.

Yvonne

Yvonne sat down and lit a cigarette. Ignoring me, she addressed herself to Nadine, unleashing a torrent of complaints. She concluded by admitting she was suicidal. She didn't trust herself and had just dropped her children off with a relative. When she left, she planned to check into the local psychiatric hospital.

"You can do that," I heard myself say. "And you should. The doctors will help you. But they can't heal you. Only Jesus can."

I spoke with absolute conviction and authority, but my mind reeled. *What are you doing? This woman is suicidal.*

Yvonne looked at me like I'd opened a wet umbrella in her face. Holding my gaze, she pulled out another cigarette before turning to Nadine.

"Who's this?"

"Patricia," Nadine smiled. "She's okay."

Yvonne lit the cigarette, took a drag, and blew it out slowly, studying me. Her eyes narrowed to black slits in the haze of smoke swirling around her head.

"You should go to the hospital," I repeated to move the conversation forward. "They'll take care of you. But Jesus can heal you."

Yvonne burst into tears. Nadine and I looked at each other. *Lord—what's going on?* We were out on a limb with a fragile soul. But Yvonne composed herself, wiping her eyes and snuffing out her

Yvonne composed herself, wiping her eyes and snuffing out her cigarette in the ashtray. Unexpectedly, she reached for my hands across the table. "Pray for me," she pleaded.

cigarette in the ashtray. Then, unexpectedly, she reached for my hands across the table.

"Pray for me," she pleaded.

I took her hands and wondered if the apostles ever felt as overwhelmed as I did in such moments. They spoke plainly and concisely in the name of Jesus. I followed their example.

Whatever I prayed, I've forgotten. But when I looked up, Yvonne sat serenely, eyes closed, holding my hands. Several seconds passed before she opened her eyes, squeezed my hands, and thanked me.

Then she was off—with a promise to drive straight to the hospital and keep us posted. We bid her goodbye and exhaled. Now Nadine studied me, with her broad, round face and inquisitive eyes. *Maybe now's a good time to share my story.*

U-turn

I dove in, starting with the accident, the healing, the Seven Steps, and my desire to pray with others.

"I want to pray the Seven Steps," Nadine responded when I finished. "Maybe Jean-Paul too. Can you bring those books?"

"Of course," I promised, looking for my umbrella. I'd had enough excitement for one day. Clearing the table, I gave Nadine a *bisous* and assured her I'd be back soon.

The following day, Yvonne called. I didn't recognize the clear, joyful voice on the other end of the line, laughing and repeating, "I'm like you now! I'm like you!" The chain-smoking, suicidal woman of yesterday, a walking nervous breakdown, was now a windmill of words. After verifying the caller was indeed Yvonne, I asked her to slow down. If I understood correctly, she had met Jesus.

Yvonne only slowed slightly, and I listened as fast as I could. After leaving Nadine and me for the hospital, she had a compelling urge to read the Bible. She pulled into a shopping center and asked a passing stranger if he knew where she could buy one. The stranger pointed straight ahead—Yvonne was parked in front of a Christian bookstore. In northern France, where few Christian bookstores existed, this was a miracle in itself.

Yvonne entered the shop and asked for a Bible. The shopkeeper suggested a version, asking if she knew how to begin. Yvonne shook her head no, and the man added some literature, asking if she belonged to a church. Again, Yvonne shook her head no, and he gave her a list of local churches. Finally, he asked if she knew Jesus. On her third no, the shopkeeper introduced Yvonne to her Healer.

Yvonne never made it to the hospital. Making a U-turn home to her family, she burst in to tell everyone about Jesus. I celebrated with her and asked her to say in touch. When she hung up, I sat on my bed, shaking my head. Jesus continued to astonish me.

Detour

As Caron and I continued our personal explorations and women's ministry, we wanted to understand more about the roots of sin and bondages. I had read such teachings in Leanne Payne's writings, which Dr. Mullen had recommended at Fishnet. Now I wondered if her books had been translated into French, which led to my next goal: to connect with healing networks or resources in France and Belgium.

To my delight, both Neil Anderson and Leanne Payne were fairly well-known in Europe. Their ministries hosted conferences annually in various European countries, and their books were available in many languages, including French. I could recommend these to the French church. When I heard they each planned conferences within the year, I registered for both. God was answering my prayers to continue my healing journey in France, and added a partner—Caron.

We attended one Leanne Payne conference together in Belgium. This gave us the common vocabulary and experience we needed to develop ministry in Lille. By practicing what we learned with each other, we gained confidence to minister to others. Adding more books to our growing collections of healing resources—in French and English—we devoured and discussed them each Friday. One book bears mention—but I need to back up to tell its story.

Do You Dream?

As I browsed the book tables at the Fishnet conference, I paused at one with a homemade banner: "Dreams." *I can skip this table,* I thought, wondering why it was at a healing conference. An elderly gentleman stood at the table, rocking on his heels. When he saw me pause, he smiled and asked, "Do you dream?"

"Of course," I said. *Didn't everyone?*

He suggested some titles, and I nodded politely, but the Spirit nudged me. "You better buy one. You're going to need it." Curious, I bought a title he recommended and packed it for France. It turned out to be another elixir, which I discovered shortly after returning to France when the phone jarred me awake.

Sylvie, a lively young French mom I'd befriended in the church during my first term, welcomed me back, then broke into rapid-fire French. I missed most of it as I tried to shake off jetlag and switch languages. But I caught "dreams" and "You must help me."

"I don't know the first thing about dreams," I confessed, now fully awake. "But I just bought a book . . ."

I told her briefly about the dream table and the Spirit's nudge. We agreed to meet later in the day at her house for coffee. In high anticipation of what God was up to next, I jumped in the shower and dressed.

When I arrived at her apartment, Sylvie greeted me, brown eyes dancing behind wire-frame glasses, chestnut hair piled on her head. After a round of *bisous* and some quick chatter, we headed for the dining room table. We hadn't seen each other in a year but would catch up another time. God was on the move.

Coffee and biscuits were waiting on the table. But the coffee went cold and the cookies remained untouched as Sylvie reported every detail of her dreams—a series of three. The dreams spoke of a cracked foundation and sounded like warnings for the church.

I struggled to keep up in French. When Sylvie finished, she left to reheat the coffee. I nibbled a cookie, thankful for caffeine and sugar to clear my brain. Sylvie refilled our cups and sat with her big brown eyes fixed on me—my turn. I emptied my cup and began.

As bubbly a personality as Sylvie had, she was also a great listener. I shared my story of healing, deliverance, and the man at the dreams table. Sylvie sat nodding, wide eyed and silent. We were staggered to see how God connected Fishnet to France—with a dreams book to help decode Sylvie's dreams. In a culture where God frequently appeared to people in dreams, it also made sense.

Dreams had led Sylvie's husband, Jean-Luc, to Christ, and Sylvie followed a year later. I knew others with similar testimonies. In Lille's metropole, with a heavy population of people from Arab cultures, God often revealed himself through dreams. I gained respect for dreams as profound vehicles of divine communication.

Sylvie and I thought her dreams significant enough to call Howard. As it turned out, Howard and Caron were both free and lived nearby. They drove right over while Sylvie made more coffee. She poured, they listened, and we all agreed to meet with the elders—Jean-Luc, who already knew about the dreams, and Jon. In uncharted waters, we'd need all hands on deck to discern and interpret these dreams.

CHAPTER 19

Dreams, My Third Language

Ronchin, France, 1998–2006

For God does speak—now one way, now another—
though no one perceives it. In a dream, in a vision of the
night, when deep sleep falls on people as they slumber in
their beds, he may speak in their ears and terrify them
with warnings, to turn them from wrongdoing and keep
them from pride, to preserve them from the pit, their lives
from perishing by the sword.

Job 33:14–18

MEANWHILE, SYLVIE AND I LAUNCHED INTO A STUDY of dreams—biblically, scientifically, and psychologically. We learned the role of dreams in Scripture in calls, prophecy, significant events, warnings, and encouragement. Scripture revealed dreams as revelatory gifts with divine purpose. When I discovered the Hebrew root word for "dreams" is "to heal," I was hooked. The Spirit was unveiling a new aspect of healing.

Howard proposed we teach our dream study at the church. I preferred flying under the radar, as did Sylvie, but we agreed. We prayed, prepared, and trusted God for the best.

Our church community listened politely and asked us to continue the study the following Sunday, which we did. Although I'm not sure anyone knew what to do with a subject so foreign to us all, it stimulated countless conversations. We made little headway on interpreting Sylvie's dreams, now a series of seven, for the church. But we stayed alert for insights—we were already witnessing a heartbreaking deterioration in the church.

When only three families remained, we missionaries thought it best to move on—a gut-wrenching decision. Other churches in the area accompanied us as we transitioned families to other churches and moved ourselves into a city church. One pastor missionary offered to continue working with the church plant, and some of our people stayed with him.

But the church didn't survive. In 2007, its doors closed, as Sylvie's dreams had predicted. Although we never discerned the crack in the foundation, news eventually surfaced that indicated a probable cause—to be confirmed in heaven.

Dream Language

When I learned that dreams might take five years to understand, it made sense. After four years in France, I managed well but wasn't yet fluent in French. In four years, I could manage dreams— I'd simply be adding another language to my skills—one of symbols and story. I carved out time to do the work. It took years, but dream language gradually yielded to practice and study.

Symbols were the basic alphabet. The symbols told a story, with plots that could be structured. Dreams conveyed emotions, ambiance, and maybe color. And they had characters—random, startling, outlandish. They included animals, shadows, and some who spoke in foreign tongues.

As a poet, I was drawn to symbol and metaphor. My Catholic upbringing and artistic eye fostered admiration for those who employed them so creatively in the arts. The dreams book and Leanne Payne's writings taught me how to deconstruct symbols. Scripture provided a treasury of information. God often asked someone, "What do you see?" and then explained the symbol. Taking a lead from this pattern and Daniel 7:1 ("He wrote down the substance of his dream"), I wrote out my dreams prayerfully before God, telling him what I had seen. And God responded with insights and interpretations.

At first, I barely remembered my dreams, unless they were nightmarish, so I kept pen and paper on my nightstand. If I scribbled a note in the night or first thing in the morning, I remembered better. Once I was fully awake, I wrote out my dreams before they dissipated. I noted every detail I recalled, focusing on symbols, plot, emotion, and characters. In the writing, insights popped into my head.

I circled all the symbols and arranged them like puzzle pieces. What was the plot? Who were the characters, and why did they appear in my dreams? I asked God constantly for insight, building a vocabulary of symbols typical to my dreams—like the framework of a puzzle I was piecing together.[20]

Gradually, the dreams yielded their mysteries. Some made me laugh, most baffled me, but soon I realized what they indicated: my heart's landscape.

Gradually, the dreams yielded their mysteries. Some made me laugh, most baffled me, but soon I realized what they indicated: my heart's landscape. It wasn't pretty. Fears, anxieties, doubts, resentments, and unhealed wounds—everything showed up symbolically in my dreams. Once I decoded the symbols, the dreams became a mirror, reflecting my inner life, with all its complexities. Dreamwork became more like a morning examination of conscience.

Through dreams, God revealed how many emotions I'd repressed or ignored as unacceptable—to me, my culture, my family, or my church. By acknowledging these emotions and managing them according to scriptural principles, I gained emotional freedom.

---

[20] I've learned that symbols are usually personal to the dreamer, although some are universal, like houses, cars, or bicycles. Dream symbol dictionaries are somewhat helpful but can lead to false interpretations.

As John the Baptist warned, "The ax is already at the root of the trees" (Matthew 3:10). God had truly set dreams as an ax to the root of my being.

The dreams offered startling insights, warnings, or conviction, alerting me of potholes ahead if I didn't change. Unexpected characters and bizarre plotlines highlighted attitudes and behaviors I needed to correct. Some came at a critical juncture to move me forward with a sense of God's blessing. Occasionally, I had a prophetic dream, like Sylvie's, but usually my dreams were about me.

Dreams pointed out the good as well as the bad. Part of healing is owning our junk but another part affirms our identity, gifts, calls, and vocations. We are God's temple, image-bearers of Christ. God highlights these facets of our beings, calling everything he creates "good," even if we sometimes do evil.

Many dreams affirmed victories, joys, qualities I possessed, or roles I inhabited. They confirmed choices I made and offered encouragement. One dream startled me awake, heart pounding—I had murdered a character. I shot up from bed, shocked, but God calmed me.

"You were supposed to put that self to death," he explained.

As my self-awareness grew, I became alert to Satan's traps and my vulnerabilities—a defense against deception. I'm not immune to any temptation, but God has taught me to detect them more quickly. My investment in dreams was paying off.

The work requires ongoing vigilance for new wounds, failures, and sins. But dreamwork also builds intimacy with the Father. Trusting the Spirit, who knows how sin works in me, I invited him to convict me of sin and lead me into all truth (John 16:8–13).

Dreamwork forged a more honest, authentic, and functional me. The more dreamwork I did, the more my fragmented heart integrated—microhealings of spirit and emotion. My mind uncluttered like that calm lake I saw in my mind's eye during the Neil Anderson conference. As my spirit lightened, I dwelt deeply with God, utterly fascinated at how he worked.

Why Dreams?

Why did God create us to dream? Why communicate through dreams, not more directly and practically? As I worked through Scripture, the sheer volume of dream references astonished me. Someone calculated about a third of the Bible speaks about them. From the prophets to events surrounding Jesus's birth to Paul's Macedonian call, the Bible begins and ends with dreams and visions.

God is also a master theologian who sometimes spins a story in the night to bypass our waking, rational, cognitive minds and reach our hearts. In Western cultures, logic rules over emotions and intuition. Analysis trumps perception. Western culture is about the only one throughout history that dismisses dreams as insignificant, which affects the Western church. It affected us in Wattignies—in our ignorance, we couldn't discern what God was saying.

One of my biblical role models is Daniel. God gave him "knowledge and understanding of all kinds of literature and learning. And Daniel could understand visions and dreams of all kinds" (Daniel 1:17). The information spoke to my artist/writer soul. God is also an artist. He loves metaphor and symbol. They encapsulate libraries of information on eternal truths and spiritual realities, succinct as our DNA's genetic code.

God also has a great sense of story and theater. As I invited him to speak through my dreams, he wove some epics. Like a kid, I anticipated his nightly tales, baffling, delighting, or leaving me with a mystery to solve. The more I paid attention to dreams, the more elaborate they became, in Technicolor.

I once considered dreams as amusing breakfast conversation. Now I respect them as God's gift to us for essential heart work. Without dreams, I wonder how we can truly know ourselves, except perhaps through therapy. And although dreamwork ferrets out sin, I suspect its primary goal is fostering heart health. As Proverbs 4:23 urges us: "Above all else, guard your heart, for everything you do flows from it." Whether God speaks to my rational mind in English (or French) or to my imaginative mind through dreams, I want to hear him.

Holistic Ministry

As God fine-tuned my healing through dreams and shifted my paradigms, he dovetailed it with the arts. My creativity increased, which in turn helped me decode dream symbols. Sometimes dreams offered solutions for creative dilemmas.

Over the years, I collaborated with Caron, Sylvie, and a few others. We critiqued each other's dreams, attempting to interpret them especially when discerning a decision, a prophetic word, or an interpersonal conflict. If an interpretation resonated, we confirmed it. If not, we prayed and waited for more insight.

The work felt intense, at least for me, but as we gained fluency in dreams, the intensity subsided and left behind another effective tool for healing. As God gathered our hearts' fragments and reintegrated them by degrees, he taught us how to gather the fragments of other hearts.

Jesus commissioned his disciples to scatter around the world and preach, heal, deliver, and baptize (Matthew 10:7–8; 28:18–19; Luke 9:1–2; 10:1–19; Mark 16:17–18). Like the apostle Paul, I felt compelled to do this work—to set prisoners free of their physical and spiritual diseases (Luke 4:18–19). They needed no judging or criticizing, no bandages, magic wands, or secret potions. They needed Jesus. With his Spirit alive in me, I expected to be moved with compassion as Jesus was and reach out to others to heal.

The ministry kept me busy. The common criticism held that inner work was navel-gazing. Although I made time for healing and dreamwork, I considered it lab work following all the theory I'd learned. I had no time for gazing at anything except my schedule, which exploded with people requesting prayer, healing, or dream interpretation. I wondered how to manage it and understood why Jesus often withdrew to be with the Father.

God gave me eyes to see past symptomatic behaviors to the roots of dysfunction. Knowing my own roots were buried in emotional wounds, where they were demonically amplified, I ignored any criticism. Peering through people's smoke screens, I saw their hurting hearts and asked about their dreams. My compassion and accuracy in "diagnosing" spiritual disease increased significantly as the dreams revealed their startling clues.

The Great Physician heals with gentle hands and sometimes uses dreams. As I ask each patient a few questions, God guides the scalpel, separating bone from marrow, truth from error. This is the miracle Christ calls us to—holistic ministry.

CHAPTER 20

Coloring Outside the Lines
Ronchin, France, 1998–2000

*I will give you hidden treasures, riches stored in secret
places, so that you may know that I am the LORD, the God
of Israel, who summons you by name.*
Isaiah 45:3

INCREASING DEMAND MOTIVATED ME TO PERSEVERE IN
the study and practice of dream interpretation with Caron and
Sylvie. I pursued healing through conferences with Leanne
Payne and her two protégés, Mario Bergner and Andy Comisky.[21]
These conferences brought me to Paris, Belgium, the Netherlands,
and Germany and triggered more profound inner healings.

Through the American Association of Christian Counselors
(AACC), I took advantage of distance learning to earn two lay counseling certificates. Since my training had launched in an unorthodox
way—on a floor in Vermont—I decided to forego formal education.
The consensus of my counseling friends was it couldn't hurt but
wasn't necessary and would add restrictions. As some reminded me,
psychologists and psychiatrists often referred people to churches for

---

[21] Leanne Payne's ministry, Pastoral Care Ministries, gave birth to
Redeemed Lives Ministries (Mario Bergner, https://www.facebook.com/
redeemedlivesinternational) and Desert Streams/Living Waters (Andy
Comisky, www.desertstream.org, *Torrents de Vie* in French). Pastoral Care
Ministries passed to new leadership and became *Ministries of Pastoral Care*
in 2009, https://ministriesofpastoralcare.com/.

issues beyond their scope. I was coloring outside the lines, addressing spiritual movements in a person's soul with appropriate counseling insights. But I worked with Christian counselors and referred people to them when appropriate.

While the conferences and courses plugged gaps in my understanding and knowledge, praying with people taught me volumes. I continued as I had begun and would seek more education as needed. But while I gained insights, theology, and an arsenal of practical tools, I longed for hands-on practice. As usual, God had a few ideas.

Expansion

I discovered my new church envisioned a healing ministry with two branches. My new pastor and a marriage counselor hoped to create a pastoral care center to serve Flanders, an area most mission agencies neglected at the time.[22] And the church would facilitate Torrents de Vie (Living Waters), a discipleship and prayer ministry that tackled the roots of sexual and relational issues. The leadership team invited me to join them, and I readily agreed.

I met like-minded souls in Ian and Liz Clifford, British missionaries who lived in Wattignies. Liz introduced me to a regional women's prayer group—Cellules de Lydie, named for Lydia in Acts 16. The group's main goal was intercession for France, not healing, but many had faith to pray for healing. I loved the fellowship and inspirational prayer times.

The Cliffords were renovating an old farmhouse in town as a refuge for victims of domestic violence. When I met with them to tell my healing story and heart for ministry, they shared their vision. They called it Tables Ouvertes—Open Tables—a meal and discussion on healing topics. Would I like to join them?

I loved the idea and thought the Cliffords perfectly suited to their vision. Ian had the twinkle in his eye and the mischievous

---

[22] EsPass'Vie, Lille, France, https://www.temoins.com/espassvie-un-centre-chretien-de-developpement-relationnel-dans-le-nord/.

demeanor of someone who could inject humor into any situation—including existential crises. If you poked him, encouragement spilled out. Elegant Liz, tall and straight as a tulip, brought a calm, maternal demeanor into tense situations. Her scrumptious cream scones and black tea offset the grim realities we dealt with during Tables Ouvertes.

We met regularly, sometimes with another interested couple and local pastors, to brainstorm workshops and events. After creating a list and schedule, we sent invitations. With a neutral location, we hoped to draw people who might not enter a church. And with the Cliffords' renowned hospitality, their home filled each month. A brick-paved courtyard took the overflow, weather permitting.

Spiritual Gifts

At Fishnet and now in Europe, I witnessed people operating in spiritual gifts I hadn't seen before. I'd rarely heard about healing gifts, discernment of spirits, or words of knowledge. These practitioners talked about such gifts as desirable for a healing ministry. They mobilized teams of people with these gifts to create, from a human standpoint, the best possible scenarios for healing.

I considered how to build such a team and what gifts I could contribute. During my Calvary years, I'd participated in Bible studies and taken spiritual gift inventory tests. While I had a baseline knowledge about the gifts, I needed a fresh look. I turned to 1 Corinthians 12.

One verse popped out in the chapter: the plural "gifts of healing" (v. 9). What were they? Did I have any? Calvary had affirmed me in the gift of evangelism. Was evangelism rooted in healing gifts? Half the time, when I prayed for someone, they received healing. If I had a healing gift, I would expect a higher success rate. But maybe as I practiced healing, my percentages would increase.

Some were suggesting I had discernment of spirits, which I questioned. If I perceived anything, wasn't it an educated guess? Some combination of knowledge, education, and experience? Or an insight or intuition, which everyone had to some degree? But maybe they were right. Maybe God was activating new gifts in me for a new phase of ministry.

I kept digging, not to split hairs or overanalyze but to heed Paul's exhortations. He urged his young protégé Timothy not to neglect a gift (1 Timothy 4:14). And he encouraged the Corinthian Church to eagerly desire spiritual gifts, especially prophecy (1 Corinthians 14:1).

I took Paul's messages to heart and actively sought God for healing gifts—for myself and others. If I were to build a healing ministry, I'd like a team with gifts of discernment, healing, wisdom, and word of knowledge. Later I asked for prophecy, which Paul prioritized—speaking God's words to others for their "strengthening, encouraging, and comfort." Despite its abuses, the beauty of true prophecy inspired me.

As a team, we discussed these questions for months. I appreciated picking Howard's pastoral and theological brains. Since we swam in a pastoral, missional, and theological fishbowl, I needed my theological ducks in a row. So working with Howard and Pastor A, I hammered out a one-page healing vision statement that satisfied most people.[23]

The church women had other questions on healing. Caron and I needed practical theology to lead them through Scripture and build their faith.

As our network expanded, so did our ministry. Armed with *Seven Steps* booklets (in French and English) and my testimony, our first ministry model was the kitchen table. Over coffee or tea, with kids and dogs in the background, we listened and prayed.

As I experimented with healing and discernment, Caron proved to have gifts of wisdom and prophecy—an answer to prayer. She also offered hospitality—beyond meals and an open house. Caron opened her heart, listening to the most horrendous stories without judgment or criticism. She'd then speak a word of wisdom that cut to the heart of a matter.

---

[23] See Healing Vision Statement in Additional Resources.

Over the weeks, Caron and I increasingly synchronized, relishing the synergy of friendship and partnership. Each Friday we persisted in prayer. Our battles were against clichés, ignorance, and demonic strongholds—battles won with worship, prayer, and sound theology.

While I'm no longer fussed about what gift I have, I routinely ask God for all the gifts necessary in any healing prayer session. It's extraordinary—and fun—to watch God distributing gifts at will, sometimes even to the person seeking healing.

I haven't moved the needle much past my 50 percent success rate, which keeps me humble and hungry for more. The other 50 percent, elated by their healing, cared nothing

> **Our battles were against clichés, ignorance, and demonic strongholds—battles won with worship, prayer, sound theology, and coffee.**

about my metric. And like John, I had no greater joy than to help any saint walk in truth and find freedom from bondages, torment, and oppression (3 John 4; John 8:36).

Syncing with the Spirit

It was essential to keep in step with the Spirit and follow his lead. As we listened to each woman, Caron and I also listened to the Spirit. Usually we were in over our heads, feeling hopelessly inadequate as we confronted powerful spiritual forces. But we trusted God, who made us competent (2 Corinthians 3:5). He never failed to show up. A prayer or idea would often spark as we listened, and we'd pray using the *Seven Steps*. Gradually we gained skill in identifying strongholds and flushing out the enemy.

Healing stays under the radar most of the time, which suits me. While we had formal and informal structures, the unscripted scenario can unfold anytime, as it did with Jesus. *Pay attention,* I tell myself constantly. *Stay focused.*

The sensational aspect of healing and deliverance documented in the gospels and Acts taught me to follow Jesus's example. Only do what I see the Father doing (John 5:19). Use invisibility to my advantage. Keep in step with the Spirit. As Jehovah-Rapha, he's with me in every scenario, strengthening, encouraging, and comforting.

While I avoided the sensational aspect, I loved the detective work of healing. Each assignment God gave me revealed new facets of his personality, which I loved. And I gained more insight into the enemy's schemes. Prayer sessions usually ended in worship as God released supernatural gifts, expelled demons, and healed.

Trench Warfare

As I entered the Torrents de Vie leadership, I heard appalling stories of abuse, trauma, and perversion. I marveled at how predictable humans are in sin and how creative in surviving trauma and abuse. But survival tactics can develop in perverse ways, with behaviors that appalled our clients as much as us. Choked by shame, guilt, and horror, goaded by the demonic, they desperately sought escape from their torment. Substance abuse, compulsive behaviors, and suicide were the alternatives of choice.

Unprepared for the evil we encountered, I wondered how many stories I could hear in a week. But my shock turned to compassion, then anger. Like David before Goliath, my spirit bristled against the enemy, so predictably laying his traps: "Who is this uncircumcised Philistine that he should defy the armies of the living God?" (1 Samuel 17:26).

What right did Satan have to wantonly destroy people? He went for the jugular, exploited every weakness, and could be tenacious. He never tired and lied like a rug. The people we met with struggled with sins common to us all, giving him footholds to attack, oppress, torment, and plant his lies. Satan doesn't always need an entry point, but he can't strike without God's permission (Job 1:6–12). When he does, it is vicious. We likened our work to trench warfare, with horrific reminders of World War I surrounding us in Flanders—trenches, bunkers, and graveyards filled with white crosses.

God's infinite mercy and patience with these survivors was humbling. His tenacity to preserve and steer them to us changed my perspective—I no longer saw victims or monsters but human heroes caught in awful webs, trying to extricate themselves from an unseen enemy. I admired their courage and resilience. How would I have survived, given their circumstances? I wanted to hand them swords to cut themselves free.

Whatever revulsion I felt roused a fierceness to rout the enemy and raise up an army of healed saints. We needed more soldiers for this war. And no warrior is as fierce as a freed captive, who knows the enemy and knows Jesus has disarmed spiritual forces of evil (Colossians 2:15). At the cross, the demonic was no match for an informed believer in Christ. Led by the Spirit and pooling our resources, our team fought for breakthroughs. We were competing against suicide and jail sentences.

Quenching Hellfire

I taught what I learned, passing out swords of truth, "sharper than any double-edged sword . . ." (Hebrews 4:12). When people came for help, I probed for roots and listened for lies—for the enemy to tip his hand. I don't think I ever met a truly evil person—thank God. But Satan poured salt in wounds, inflamed emotions, and blinded minds.

Wounds and emotions could be healed. Sins could be forgiven. We placed a life-size cross in the sanctuary, soon covered with Post-it notes of prayer, confession, or commitments. Over and over, I quoted Jesus: "Everything is possible for one who believes" (Mark 9:23). I shared with them a prayer Leanne Payne taught, "Lord, I am capable of the monstrous and the petty. And if not for you, I would do much worse."

For the hesitant, I prayed a biblical prayer: "Lord, I do believe; help my unbelief" (Mark 9:24). For the skeptical, I prodded, "Maybe

God won't heal, but why not ask?" For those without faith, I told the story of the paralytic, whose friends ripped off a roof to lower him before Jesus (Luke 5:17–26). I offered to be that friend, lend them my faith, and accompany them to Jesus and the cross. Because of my own history, I had hope for each person who came to us.

First, we offered hope. Without excusing any behavior, we suggested where roots might be hidden and handed them tools. We called each one to dig deep, to confess sin and sinful reactions to sins against them, to become active participants in their restoration.

Second, we told our stories. Since people often put pastors and missionaries on pedestals, we shattered their illusions by bringing our skeletons out of the closet. We taught as peers—sinner to sinner, saint to saint. When we divulged our dirty little secrets, they more easily confessed theirs.

Third, we called for change, challenging them to confront their demons and overcome. Not through willpower, discipline, and psychological techniques alone but by faith in the power in Jesus's name. If he freed and healed us, he could do the same for them. We had the tools, the programs, the heart, the passion, the gifts—useless unless someone was willing to change. Some took the challenge. Too many walked away. We grieved those who quit and pressed on.

We were snatching prisoners out of hellfire (Jude 1:23), urging them to ask, seek, knock, and persist until God answered. When their hearts failed, we called them to courage. When our hearts failed, they begged us not to quit. Together, we witnessed God's electrifying power, expelling demons and collapsing mindsets. However sordid and hopeless a session began, it usually ended with a breakthrough. And we celebrated every millimeter of victory.

The sea of pain we encountered in Lille threatened to drown us. But God's ocean of love displaced the pain. He renewed our strength and poured out graces. As my awareness and skill increased, I created three-legged stools for others. The work was dangerous and fun, exhausting and exhilarating. It never stopped—and neither did God.

CHAPTER 21

Calls and Hungers
Ronchin, France, 1998–2000

*Then the LORD said to Moses, "See, I have chosen
Bezalel . . . and I have filled him with the Spirit of God,
with wisdom, with understanding, with knowledge and
with all kinds of skills—to make artistic designs for work
in gold, silver and bronze, to cut and set stones, to work in
wood, and to engage in all kinds of crafts."*
Exodus 31:1–5

WHILE THIS TUMULTUOUS MINISTRY GREW, I searched for ways to decompress from its intensity. God gave grace for the impossible tasks he called us to and placed me among stout-hearted teammates. But he also gave gifts of beauty to survive the ugly—arts and writing.

How God planned to combine the ingredients he'd sprinkled into my life—art, healing, missions, writing, and dreams—was a mystery but emerging. At the least, creative gifts were spiritual oxygen for me, and I could pass the oxygen tank to others as needed.

Restoring the Gifts

God had already introduced me to Leanne Payne, a writer and C. S. Lewis scholar at Wheaton College. Although I never met her, Payne mentored me in the arts through her books and lectures. She taught on the imagination, ritual, symbol, and poetic awe—topics that reverberated in my soul. Her teaching on "the holy Christian imagination" arrested me. I'd never heard the imagination described as holy—only fickle, unreliable, and not to be indulged.

Payne's understanding of the arts, artists, and their role in the church created a theological framework for me. She inspired me to think more biblically about the arts and affirmed the artistic call. Her life-giving teachings brought me, as C. S. Lewis wrote in *The Weight of Glory*, "the scent of a flower we have not found, the echo of a tune we have not heard, news from a country we have never yet visited."[24]

Into this fertile soil, God dropped a key verse in my lap—from Paul's prayer in Ephesians 1:15–23. Although the Ephesians were a mature body of believers, he urged them to see with the eyes of the heart "so that you may know him better" (Ephesians 1:17). I adopted Paul's prayer, asking God to open the eyes of my heart. I needed to rethink creativity and the imagination. Without them, I'd miss the riches God had in store for me. My image of God would be malformed, and I'd struggle to survive the ministry.

Restoring the Broken Imagination

While I had a strong imagination, it was broken, polluted, and suppressed. It envisioned catastrophes, negative reactions, and worst-case scenarios. Pornography seared it. Scary films haunted it. I didn't consider the imagination vital for Christian life but a hindrance. It conformed more to "the pattern of this world," and unless I renewed it, I'd miss the transformation I sought (Romans 12:2).

I pulled out the big guns: my *Strong's Concordance*, commentaries, and a Greek word study New Testament. With highlighters, colored pencils, and Post-it notes, I added color, tags, and doodles to my Bible. Starting with Paul's phrase "eyes of the heart," I cracked open my word study New Testament. The phrase was translated from one Greek word, *dianoia,* into English as "imagination," "intellect,"

---

[24] C. S. Lewis, *The Weight of Glory, and Other Addresses* (New York: Macmillan and Co., 1966), 4–5.

"mind," or "understanding" (Matthew 22:37; Luke 1:51; Ephesians 1:18; 4:18; Hebrews 8:10).[25]

I traced *dianoia* through the New Testament. When I read Jesus's first and greatest commandment, I underlined, highlighted, and starred it: "Love the Lord your God with all your heart and with all your soul and with all your mind [*dianoia*]" (Matthew 22:37; Mark 12:30; Luke 10:27). According to the Greek dictionary and lexical aides, that included my thoughts, understanding, and imagination. Paul used the metaphor of the eyes. Could I equally use the metaphor "mind of the heart?" To love God, I needed to love him with my cognitive mind and my imaginative mind.

I wrote *dianoia* in the margin, circled it, and pondered it for months. How open were the eyes of my heart? How clear was my spiritual vision?

The imagination, damaged in the fall, needs restoration. The world, the flesh, and the devil corrupt it. Trauma, violence, and occult practices sear it. How could I clean up my two minds? How could I cultivate my imagination?

When asked how to cope with unimaginable abuse, one rape victim attested, "Only beauty helps." She spent hours in gardens. A colleague's son was murdered. She survived the shock in art museums, where abstract expressionism gave voice to her grief.[26]

These women experienced what Scripture teaches: the importance of beauty and guarding what our eyes see. I followed their examples. Gardens and art museums became places of visual renewal.

My camera accompanied me everywhere. Through its lens, I studied color, form, texture, expression. I brought flowers into the house more frequently. Delighting in their beauty and fragrance, I drew or painted them or composed poems about them. The arts

---

[25] Spiros Zodhiates, ThD, *The Complete Word Study New Testament* (Chattanooga: AMG Publishers, 1991), 891.
[26] Dr. Dianne B. Collard, *I Choose to Forgive* (Eugene: Wipf and Stock, Cascade Books, 2018).

and beauty became a way to restore my imagination, love God, and worship him more fully.

Restoring my imagination meant purging my mind of thoughts and images from the pornography I was exposed to as a kid. The explicit billboards between France and Belgium didn't help, nor did most French films. My litmus test was Philippians 4:8–9: thinking on whatever was true, noble, right, pure, lovely, admirable, excellent, and praiseworthy. To reduce the cultural barrage of pollution, I monitored what I watched and restricted my viewing to beautiful films—visually and thematically. Eventually I gave away my TV. I prayed as I passed every billboard and practiced the psalmist's discipline to "set no worthless thing before my eyes" (Psalm 101:3 NASB).

Cultivating the imagination took discipline and is somewhat subjective. What worked for me might not work for another. What makes something beautiful? For years, I've asked this question in many cultures. Some consider visual beauty second to sound, word, or behavior, as in the southern American expression "Don't be ugly."

Though I started with my thought life and eyes, I had to wash my ears clean with beautiful music and "cleanse my palate" with healthier food. Revisiting the book of Daniel, I wondered if his diet connected to the wisdom God gave him and his friends. Were they able to understand dreams better because they maintained healthier diets? A diet free of fats, sugar, and chemicals cleared my mind considerably, which helped with writing. But I noticed my dreams changing, with less grotesque images, less frightening plots. Maybe eating pizza late at night does influence our dreams.

Beauty and the arts created the oxygen I needed for ministry. Before beginning a tough session, I walked a park. Afterward, I evacuated the horrible stories with worship music. I brought my solutions into ministry—images and objects for people to express themselves—my first forays into art therapy. Later I added paint and paper, asking people to write or draw what they couldn't voice. Sometimes I'd take them to a garden, the coast, or an art show.

With the discoveries came more questions. God had more intention for me with the arts. What was it?

Reframing My Call

As I explored more options to decompress, I read a notice for a three-week picture framing class in the city's downtown shopping mall. Curious because my father framed art, I signed up to try my hand. Besides, if I became an artist, I'd need frames.

But this wasn't your local craft store framing. Professional French framing is an art form, requiring a university degree. It brings elaborate matting solutions to framing styles, most of which I'd never seen. Hooked, I extended my three-week class over months.

During one class, I cut my finger with a mat knife—a deep and bloody slice. I jumped back from the worktable to protect my project, and the teacher ran over with the first-aid kit. Sitting in a corner with a rag wrapped around my finger, I studied my classmates. Their artwork dazzled me. Their focus, skill, and framing choices inspired me. Hunched over their creations, they were oblivious to all else. As I admired them, the Spirit spoke.

"Do you see these people?"

"Yes, Lord," I sighed. "Look at the beauty they're creating. I love them, and I love what they're doing."

"That's because you're one of them. You're an artist. And these are the people I'm sending you to. They would no more enter a church than the church would enter their studios. They're an unreached people group—your people."

It was a defining moment—a collision of call and vocation. Without hesitation, while the instructor bandaged my finger, I said yes. It would be a joy.

A few days later I read Frederick Buechner's words: "The place God calls you to is the place where your deep gladness and the world's deep hunger meet."[27] I couldn't believe God would use my love of the arts to meet the world's deep hunger. But what a thrill—my niche!

Call established, I tackled the "how." How would I meet the world's deep hunger with art? What was my place of service—in mission or not? It never occurred to me (or anyone in my world) to combine art and mission. Before the internet spawned the current creative age, the Protestant Church rarely engaged the arts. The arts languished as idolatry or ornament except for worship music and stained-glass windows. A few artists were pioneering arts in mission, but another decade would pass before a global arts movement ignited.

> "The place God calls you to is the place where your deep gladness and the world's deep hunger meet."

Bezalel had all kinds of creative skills. I didn't have skills but could acquire them. Daniel, skilled in dreams and literature, worked in government. Was my niche still in missions?

These internal migrations intersected another one I'd soon make. Just before Christmas in 2000, my brother Paul called. Our father was losing his battle with lung cancer. It was time to come home.

[27] Frederick Buechner, "Vocation," Frederick Buechner website (blog post), July 18, 2017, https://www.frederickbuechner.com/quote-of-the-day/2017/7/18/vocation.

CHAPTER 22

A Bleak Midwinter
Pawcatuck, CT, December 2000–March 2001

The cords of death entangled me, the anguish of the grave
came over me; I was overcome by distress and sorrow.
Psalm 116:3

I HUNG UP THE PHONE IN SHOCK AND DISSOLVED IN TEARS. *We thought Dad had more time—treatments had progressed so well.* Now the doctors gave Dad a month at best, terminating treatment and recommending hospice care. In disarray, I knelt on the floor and prayed between sobs—*Please keep Dad alive until I get home.*

But I had to think. It was Saturday, two days before Christmas. Trains and planes would be packed and expensive—if seats were still available. I'd have to hold mail, stop utilities . . . *for how long?* The banks were closed. *Do I have enough cash for travel?* I checked my wallet, then called Howard and Caron.

We talked over options, responsibilities, and logistics, and they offered to drive me to whatever airport I needed. I rifled through my agenda as we spoke, rattling off names, dates, meetings, and phone numbers—we decided who to call, what to delegate, and what to cancel. Howard would pass the word to the church. With a game plan in place, I hung up and booked a flight.

I pulled out a suitcase and threw things in while adding more items to my mental checklist: *Clean the fridge. Leave plants with neighbors. Call someone to pick me up in New York.*

By the grace of God (and the Moores), I left within twenty-four hours. The flight was uneventful and my seat mercifully private. Wrapping the flimsy airline blanket around me, I curled up and cried my eyes out. My flight hostess left me to it, discretely delivering food, water, and tissues as needed.

My youngest brother, Peter, picked me up in New York. We hugged and shed a few tears, then scurried from airport to car in the frigid air. Steaming cups of Starbucks fogged the windows from their cupholders, candy canes hooked to their sides. Soothing Enya Christmas music played as he turned the ignition. With hand sanitizer and tissues in the console, I could always count on Peter for a ride with artistic flair.

We inched our way north through traffic onto I-95. Mom and Dad lived in southeastern Connecticut, three hours away. We took our time and arrived for dinner.

The house was full and chaotic—it was Christmas Eve. Mom banged around in the kitchen until dinner was ready. Siblings, partners, kids, and in-laws crowded in the open living/dining area, laughing, talking, playing. As I entered, someone sitting with Dad on the couch rose immediately and motioned me to take his place. Dad had a bulky bandage on his head, and I stopped in my tracks.

"Oh, we should have warned her . . ." he said to Mom, touching the bandage and apologizing. I wanted to hug him, but how fragile was he? We embraced gently and held hands while Paul and Tom set up folding chairs and tables to accommodate everyone. When the kitchen crew transported fragrant dishes from kitchen to table, Allen moved Dad to his wheelchair.

Numb from travel and emotions, I excused myself as soon as we finished eating. Mom led me to a nearby bedroom, where I passed out to the ongoing family chatter.

Beauty in Brokenness

I woke in the morning to Dad's appalling cough. So began the painful journey of accompanying him through his last weeks. We made the best of our bittersweet Christmas, thankful for one more. Avoiding the hard questions, we ate breakfast, took our showers, and dressed. Then Paul brought out gifts, including a scarf for Dad. I teared up—how long would he need it?

In the late afternoon, Dad and I enjoyed a private moment in the legendary Butler Reading Hour. This tradition evolved as we came of age and began pulling away from family. Dad appealed to us—could we not gather for Sunday dinner and catch up with one another? With groans and eye rolls, we agreed. When we hit drinking age, Dad sweetened the deal by offering one of his signature cocktails. In winter, he built a fire in the fireplace, another magnet to draw us.

When our sister-in-law, Maureen, entered the family, unaware that reading didn't count as conversation, she opened a book and read until dinner. We looked at one another, then Dad, strangely silent. Seizing the moment, we grabbed the nearest book or magazine, and the Butler Reading Hour was born.

To this day, in any Butler gathering, as 5:00 p.m. approaches, we close devices, finish errands, or emerge from naps. Someone offers to make cocktails. We grab snacks and reading material and settle in for a read, nibble, and sip until dinner.

This Christmas, I returned from a walk, and Dad waved me over. He wanted to show me one of his gifts—a photo book documenting explorer Ernest Shackleton's Antarctic expedition.[28] Its story of survival and endurance hit home. During the weeks to come, we'd undergo both. But this evening, we forgot our troubles, poring over the stunning photography. In classic Dad style, he pointed us to beauty and courage in the face of suffering, by which we would all survive.

Hospice and Lifelines

The day after Christmas, we thudded back to reality. A hospice nurse arrived to review end-of-life options with us, interrupted by our

---

[28] Caroline Alexander, *The Endurance: Shackleton's Legendary Antarctic Expedition*, (New York: Knopf, 1998).

intermittent meltdowns. We voted unanimously to keep Dad home with hospice care. Although we were unprepared for the invasion of people and equipment the following morning, we soon welcomed their arrival. Paul and I moved in, and our siblings rotated through weekends to relieve us and visit Dad. A hospice nurse would arrive as Paul left for work during the week and leave when he returned. Mom and I handled the domestic front.

Mornings dawned with Dad's coughing and a knock on the door—the hospice nurse. While she bathed and dressed Dad, Mom and I prepared breakfast and set the table. When the nurse wheeled him out, we put gloves on his cold hands and wrapped his new scarf around his neck. He sipped tea as we ate and made small talk. The oxygen machine hissed and droned in the background, its spaghetti cords splayed around the house.

The hospice people taught us how to manage Dad's care, and God's grace held us. As Dad declined, they brought in one piece of equipment after another. Outside the windows, plump red cardinals cheered us from the bird feeder. After dinner, we fed Dad chocolate mints and played his favorite music. And as each exhausting day ended, we watched a jazz series, falling asleep one by one.

God strengthened me to survive this awful period by pointing out a creative outlet in town. While running an errand one afternoon, I passed a brightly painted shop—Get Fired Up, a paint-your-own-pottery shop. I stopped to investigate and stayed for an hour, painting to peaceful music. When I left, I felt like a new woman. From then on, I'd leave Mom with the hospice nurse as often as possible and run into town to paint a pot, plate, or mug. In a bleak season, the colors and music revived me.

Another lifeline was nearby Enders Island—the home of a Catholic retreat center—one of our parents' favorite places. Mom and I frequently drove over for a walk. Taking the single-lane causeway to its campus, we entered its unique world, with a sacred art institute, tiny stone chapel, and bookshop. We didn't talk much, wrapped to our eyeballs against the cold, leaning into the bracing wind.

One weekend in January, Peter drove up, and we slipped out after an early morning snowfall. Dad was deteriorating rapidly, and we were suffocating in grief. Outside, a winter wonderland beckoned. We bundled up, left the family, and stepped out into the snowy silence. With the dry air sucking oxygen from our lungs, we hurried to start the car, scrape the windows, and jump in, shivering till the heat kicked in. As we drove into town, we thought we might find a church to attend but ended up driving aimlessly. Then inspiration struck.

"I know what we need," I said. "Enders Island."

Peter turned the wheel without a word. As we crossed the causeway, the snowstorm weakened into flurries. By the time we parked, the sun was peeking out over a world encased in ice.

Death and Legacy

We walked the crusted snow under the weak sun and sheltered from the wind in the chapel. While Peter knelt at the altar, I sat in a pew and stared at the guttering candles. My gaze wandered to the intricate wood tracings and stained-glass windows. One winked at me from a high arch as the sun peeked through. I looked up—the Lamb of God, standing with a victory banner, filled a quatrefoil. Sunlight flared, blinding me momentarily.

"It's your turn," the Spirit whispered.

My turn?

"Time for you to take up the arts—your inheritance from your father. He's dying."

I looked at Peter, the other artist in our family. *But Lord, I'm the writer.*

"Follow me."

Two weeks later, Dad was gone. The coroner arrived within the hour, wrote the death certificate, and whisked him away while we sobbed in the next room. Hospice swept in next, removing all equipment—all traces of our hospice journey. We never again saw the hospice workers who had accompanied and consoled us for six weeks.

On a gray day with flurries, we trundled off to meet the funeral director for the grisly task of choosing a coffin. After that chore, Mom called the parish priest while Peter and I wrote the obituary. Over lunch we planned the funeral and took turns notifying people. Neighbors discretely deposited casseroles on the deck.

The wake was loud and packed with friends, relatives, and neighbors. Crowding in to pay their respects, they cheered us with family lore, a fond memory, or one of Dad's exploits. We shared tears and laughter. The funeral, by contrast, was a solemn affair that reduced us to puddles.

We took the ferry across the sound to Long Island for the burial, huddled in the warm cabin to avoid the biting wind. As we approached the shore, all eyes turned to the darkening sky—a blizzard. Arriving in its full fury, our caravan crawled behind the hearse as it skidded to the cemetery. We passed accidents and cars abandoned in ditches. At the cemetery entrance, we stared at two hearses that had collided.

How exactly did a graveside funeral happen in a blizzard? As quickly as possible. The staff led us to a pavilion where the wind and snow whipped through sideways. We declined the funeral director's invitation to sit on the metal folding chairs, wrapped in faux fur wrappings, hopelessly soaked. Instead, we stood and shivered until the service completed, then fled to our cars.

"It's your turn," the Spirit whispered.

My turn?

"Time for you to take up the arts—your inheritance from your father. He's dying."

At a nearby tavern, we thumped the snow off our coats and boots and thawed out before a crackling fire. "And that," we declared, "should never happen again."

A Clock Ticking

After Dad died, I stayed with Mom for three months in the house, which now felt as silent and empty as a tomb. No more hospice workers or family members. No hiss or drone of oxygen. In the living room, the antique clock ticked like a professional mourner.

Mom wasn't one for emotion. Never a great talker, she spoke even less in her grief. Ever the practical nurse, she began purging Dad's belongings the day after the funeral. As she purged, I wailed and pulled things out of the trash—"Not this, Mom!" We compromised with a commitment to collaborate, call the siblings to collect whatever mementos they wanted, and donate the rest to thrift stores.

When flowers arrived late that first morning, I inhaled their fragrance deeply, grateful for their beauty. Mom and I kept up our walks on Enders Island, sometimes stopping for lunch at a local restaurant. As often as possible, I went to Get Fired Up to paint. And Mom adjusted to widowhood by learning to pump gas and test the well water.

When I could find words, I wrote a newsletter to friends, churches, and supporters—not many knew I was home. I described my father's illness and death, my time with Mom now, and the weight of decisions before us. It sparked a heartwarming outpouring of love, affirmation, and prayer—the most memorable from Paul, a few weeks later on my birthday.

He and I traveled to Mary's house for a quiet celebration. He handed me an unlikely gift—two books on the writer's craft. I looked at him in surprise. Books? From the nonreader, builder, contractor, sports junkie, and father of four?

"You missed your calling," he said. "That prayer letter . . ." And choking up, he walked away.

But his words ricocheted through my spirit as from God. Paul was also a mentor and encourager, like Dad. I took the treasure to bed and thanked God for him, his gift, and another encouragement to write.

As the weeks wore on, competing pressures jostled inside me: Do I stay with Mom or return to France? I hated to leave Mom alone, but what about the call to France? I was torn between Luke 14:26 and 1 Timothy 5:8. Do I leave family or provide for family? It was too early for Mom to decide what she wanted to do, and I didn't want to rush her. But I didn't want to close out of France if she moved in with someone else in the family.

The antique clock ticked off the pros and cons each evening as we ignored our conundrums: if and when I left for France, if and when Mom moved. We couldn't resolve those issues—shattered in grief.

One evening after retiring to my upstairs bedroom, which doubled as Dad's office, I sat at his drafting table. Pencils and pens jammed empty mustard tins and cheese jars. Framing instruments mixed with his late brother's engineering tools. In the center sat a stack of papers—Dad's genealogy work.

I poked through the titles on the small bookshelf he had built into the wall. A thin pamphlet caught my eye, "Letter to Artists" by Pope John Paul II. Intrigued, I curled up in bed to read, and two Billy Graham pamphlets fell out. They were stamped with the 1957 crusade at Madison Square Garden, which I guessed Dad would have attended.

How Dad merged his staunch Catholicism with evangelist Billy Graham, I never knew. Now the tracts were bookmarks for a papal encyclical, which felt like a wink from God. The pamphlet helped me further integrate the artist's call and vocation. I packed it for my return to France, which I had decided to do. I needed to move on—at least until Mom made her decision.

CHAPTER 23

Hot Bug Summer

Hamden, CT, July–September 2001

Be still, and know that I am God.
Psalm 46:10

MY RETURN WOULD BE SHORT-LIVED. AFTER FOUR years in France, I was due to start a year of home ministry assignment (HMA) in the fall. I debated the wisdom of traveling back and forth, but grief won. I couldn't imagine attempting ministry in Lille's gloomy winter, grieving where no one knew Dad. How could I talk about him? I needed my home tribe—family, friends, and church—with whom to commiserate.

On the other hand, an HMA would challenge me—a year of church visits and presentations. Withdrawing to France for a few months to my own place, working, and seeing my French tribe would be therapeutic. The months would allow me time to make arrangements to suspend ministry for a year and return to the States. And I could process and pray with Caron.

As I set my departure from Lille for July 2001, I checked my visa. It would expire before I returned in 2002—a gap of two weeks. I stopped by the immigration office. Could I renew in Lille?

My contact at immigration nodded and tucked my dossier in her desk drawer. With a conspiratorial wink, she patted the drawer and said, "Come see me when you're back." She would personally oversee my file. I nodded back—a mistake that cost me dearly.

Hot Bugs

As I exited LaGuardia airport into New York's steamy humidity, a wall of sound stopped me in my tracks: katydids, cicadas, and crickets. We called them hot bugs. How I missed their chorus. Along with the Manhattan skyline and a cluster of taxis outside the airport, they welcomed me home.

Tom and Peter waited for me to collect myself, then steered me through taxis and traffic to the car. As we escaped New York's congestion, retreating to Oyster Bay, I let the music wash my weary soul. I'd returned to my roots—the source, the French would say. In its rich soil, we'd walk a year of grief with beaches and boat rides in the bay of our childhood. Already I felt better.

After a few days, I moved up to Hamden, Connecticut, to live with Mary and Brian and their two kids, Stephanie and Matthew. Stephanie, my spiritual daughter, was our miracle child, having survived a traumatic birth. In response to our prayers, Stephanie exceeded all expectations and grew into a beautiful, book-loving night owl and Irish dancer.

Matt, no less a miracle, started life with a bumpy year of chronic ear infections. By preschool he was in and out of ER and medical offices with asthma and pneumonia. Now eight years old, Matt flitted from one end of the house to another, our empath and joy bug, with a ready smile and quirky sense of humor.

I looked forward to seeing their new home, which would be my base for a year of travel. The McLaughlins lived in a central location to the churches and people I'd be visiting. Since my sister didn't work outside the home, we'd steal spare moments between our schedules for a coffee. Sometimes Mom would join us, or we'd drive to see her, or I'd stay with her for a week.

The year offered me a rare chance to build relationship with the kids, as Uncle Leo had built one with me. When I was with them, I'd tuck them in with Bible stories and prayers, answering all their questions about France. We'd walk down the street for candy or ice cream, listening to the mockingbirds, counting their songs. Stephanie and I renewed our introverted deep girl talks. And I cuddled with Matt on the couch, watching reruns of Star Wars.

Deep Listening

On our first night together, the McLaughlins and I ate dinner in the summer room. We chattered away until I put my fork down, which triggered an exodus. Everyone bolted from the table, whisking away their plates and cups. I sat astonished. After seven years in France, I had acquired the habit of lingering over a meal with conversation. I'd forgotten the speed and commotion of the American lifestyle. As the notoriously slow eater in the family, I tested their patience.

"What about conversation?" I asked as the family cleared the table. "What about the hot bugs? Don't you want to listen to them?"

No takers. Mary loaded the dishwasher while Brian headed for the den to queue the television programming. The kids disappeared.

"Okay then," I announced, bringing my dishes in, too, "I'll be outside if anyone wants to join me."

I dragged a lawn chair into the backyard and sat spellbound in a concert of songbirds, peepers, and hot bugs. Sunset, another of my addictions, threw pink streamers around the sky, and its humid air stuck to my skin. The family checked on me now and then, puzzled or amused. In the heat, Mary reminded me to "drink some water." Stephanie wandered out, listened a moment, and disappeared again. A few minutes later, Matt flitted over, all questions.

"What about the mosquitoes? Aren't you hot?"

"I'm listening to the hot bugs, Matt."

"What are hot bugs? What color are they? Do they bite?"

How to explain reverse culture shock to an eight-year-old? I had no words, and an eight-year-old only waits so long. I assured him all was well, and he jumped on his bike to find friends.

Undisturbed now, I sat in the twilight choir, letting my thoughts meander while my spirit caught up with all the transitions. As I listened to the bugs, their drone mixed with my thoughts: *Stay out of the sun. Drink plenty of water. Avoid unnecessary activity. Resist the performance trap—*

I only do what I see the Father doing.[29]

Wait, what? Was that me or—I sat up, straining to penetrate the hot bug chorale to hear the still small voice. Jesus had entered the conversation.

"Be still and know that I am God. The lilies of the field toil not."[30]

Neither did these peepers, cicadas, crickets, and katydids.

"Yet your heavenly Father feeds them"[31]—those who chirped, droned, and whirred around me.

I pushed aside a vague guilt that I wasn't being productive and wouldn't cut it in America. I couldn't justify my behavior to anyone but couldn't resist the hot bugs. Through them, I heard God—the most productive activity I did all summer. Until this moment, I didn't know what to do. I knew what the schedule looked like and the expectations and obligations awaiting me. I'd move through my paces, regardless of grief. But that was the external story. The internal story was deciding which of the forking roads ahead of me to take. Sitting in the darkness, I was piercing a dark night of the soul.

Should I resign from missions and live with Mom or continue in France? Could I attempt a creative career in the States, or was I destined to pioneer arts in mission? I would only know by hearing from God. He understood my longings. After ten years of constant transition, Jesus encouraged me to sit, rest, and be still. Listen to the hot bugs. The answers would come.

The Still Point of Summer

Listening set the pace for my year ahead. In a few weeks, the temps would drop, and the hot bugs would depart. The invitations could wait. I blocked August to unpack, create presentations, and brace for a heavy fall schedule.

---

[29] John 5:19
[30] Psalm 46:10; Matthew 6:28
[31] Matthew 6:26

After ten years of constant transition, Jesus encouraged me to sit, rest, and be still. Listen to the hot bugs. The answers would come.

In the meantime, it was summer—a time for vacation, sitting around a pool, listening for the ice cream truck, and playing with the kids, always good medicine. Temps soared into triple digits—a record-breaking heatwave. We lounged by the pool and sweltered, dipping in and out to cool off. Even the neighborhood dogs were too hot to bark.

Stephanie lounged with us on lawn chairs, riveted to our every conversation. Matt and his buddies cavorted in the pool. Lawnmowers tossed the scent of fresh-cut grass into the air, and flowers populated every yard. When Brian put an air conditioner in the master bedroom, I holed up there to watch videos for my first lay counseling course.

But September was coming. I made calls, responded to emails, and ordered cards and brochures. On Labor Day, Brian covered the pool, the mockingbirds left, and the hot bug chorale faded to a wheeze. My autumn activities were about to start, and the kids would begin school. But we never forgot hot bug summer. It entered the family lore as one of our favorites.

Fall Forward

My second home ministry assignment intrigued me—what did God intend? Although my plans included family time, personal development, visits with friends, supporting churches, and prayer partners, anything could happen. I'd be traveling all over New York and New England.

But as my network evolved, it took me further still. Looking for ministry partners, resources, and inspiration, I wanted to investigate a few arts ministries and like-minded churches. I also hoped to attract artists into cross-cultural work. Researching writer's groups and conferences, I registered for one conference in Hartford.

On the healing front, I planned to attend another Fishnet Conference with Donna and explore healing ministries in New England. Later in the year, funded by complete strangers, I scheduled flights to attend Schools of Healing Prayer with Christian Healing Ministries in Jacksonville, FL. And researching local art therapists, I scheduled an appointment with one to process grief with her.

But my plans were the external story. The internal story was about to unfold.

Three Affirmations

Pastor A and I met for breakfast one Sunday before church, catching up over pancakes, eggs, and coffee. From France and missions to Calvary Church and family news, we didn't waste a minute. I shared God's sequel to my blockbuster healing—Sylvie's dreams, Yvonne, the arts, and writing. Before we left, we set a date to meet in a month. In the meantime, Pastor A gave me homework—to write something and send it to him.

"On healing?" I asked.

"Not necessarily. Anything you like."

I mulled over the essay I'd written on hot bugs. Or maybe my next prayer letter. *But why not on healing?*

"I could send you an essay," I decided.

"Great—send it along. Also, think about carrying a notebook with you to capture thoughts—an idea journal."

I pulled mine out of my bag and showed him. He nodded approvingly, paid the bill, and we left for church. On arrival, I bumped into a good friend and supporter. After hugs and greetings, she told me she'd been praying for me and believed God had given her a word for me. Did I want to hear it?

"Of course," I responded.

"What are you doing with your writing?"

My eyes brimmed with tears.

"Were you eavesdropping?" I asked.

In answer to her bewildered expression, I recounted my breakfast with Pastor A, ending with my assigned homework. Now her eyes filled. We prayed briefly as people flowed into the pews around us, John and Jessie Barney among them, smiling and waving at us.

"You write the best prayer letters I've ever read, even in my agency," John boomed.

Whoa, Lord—three affirmations in one morning?

If I knew nothing else, I knew this was an answer—the fork in the road to take. With these affirmations and allies, I eagerly awaited the upcoming writer's conference. But before the week was out, the inconceivable rocked our world, disrupting every American life.

CHAPTER 24

Scribes, Mentors, and a Walnut Tree

Hamden, CT, 2001–2002

*There is a time for everything, and a season for every
activity under the heavens.*
Ecclesiastes 3:1

F OR THOSE WHO LIVED THROUGH IT, 9/11 IS A DATE
etched in the psyche. As people reunited in the following
days and weeks, the question "Where were you?" went viral.
Tom, Allen, and Peter still lived on Long Island, and Peter and I
had recently been to the World Trade Towers for customs. But on
9/11, we were in Maine for a family reunion.

My parents' anniversary was September 10. Two years prior,
we celebrated their fiftieth wedding anniversary in Maine, where
they had honeymooned and loved to vacation. This year, in Dad's
honor, we booked a week in their favorite inn. What we intended
as a healing time turned to trauma as the horrific images scrolled
on television screens.

We had scattered around Boothbay Harbor but regathered at
the inn one by one as we caught the news. A flurry of phone calls
followed to check on family and friends, then we met for lunch and
talked over plans—stay or head home? Paul and Maureen left early.
Those of us who stayed found a local chapel holding a prayer service
and knelt on the floor with others.

Once home, we sat glued to the television like most people.
Within days, the anthrax scare hit close to Hamden. I rescheduled

a flight to Florida. Calls came in from my French team and friends. In our national trauma, I thanked God for arranging my life to be with family but far from Manhattan. And as life settled down, I rebooted my schedule.

Scribes and Scribblers

Two women from two different supporting churches each invited me to their writer's groups in Massachusetts. I accepted and visited both. Since they were each an hour's drive from Hartford, I could only manage one and chose Scribes and Scribblers in Springfield, Massachusetts.

We met in a restaurant, ordering pizza, pub food, desserts, or coffee—whatever suited needs and appetites. I loved the support, camaraderie, and professionalism of the group. And the long commutes provided time to catch up with my friend, prayer partner, and fellow writer.

The group met monthly. Everyone who desired a critique could bring a piece of writing and sign up. My first submission was my hot bugs essay, "The Healing Power of Hot Bugs." It earned positive critiques and an invitation to submit it to the group's monthly newsletter. *Not bad,* I thought. *I like this.*

Impatient for each month to pass, I never failed to submit something for critique. My year in the States would fly fast, and I wanted to maximize my time with the group's wisdom and experience. With one professional editor and several published writers critiquing, I made steady progress. If they deemed one of my pieces strong enough to submit for publication, they suggested a market. When I followed their advice, my submissions sold.

This is easy, I thought, although I'd revise that statement now. But I learned an important lesson: my chances of acceptance would increase if I matched my submission to the market. A month later, at my first writer's conference in Hartford, the facilitator reinforced the lesson. He taught on craft and the publishing industry, urging us to be diligent in both. To ignore the industry would mark us as amateurs and doom our submissions to the circular file (the trash basket).

The facilitator insisted we call ourselves writers and not dither about whether we were writers if we hadn't published. If we wrote, we were writers. If we didn't write, we might fall into depression, alcoholism, or toxic behaviors. I called myself a writer from then on.

As for diligence, I bought *The Christian Writer's Market Guide* and pored over it several times a week. And with no idea what I might produce, I set my writing practice at ten hours a week, two hours each evening. If I had an evening meeting, I wrote when I returned home or later in the week. I adjusted for circumstances but stuck to the practice until I formed a writing habit.

By the time I reentered France the following summer, the habit was an addiction. I couldn't wait to open my computer each evening. Writing longhand or tapping on a keyboard, I filled notebooks and hard drives with poems, essays, and stories. When blogs emerged, I blogged. I loved the ease of writing in my mother tongue, not alternating between two languages.

The year laid the foundations for my journey as a writer. I embraced the call, identity, and confirmations. Dipping my toes into the industry, I built a network and earned my first publication credits. I had books on craft and a writer's market guide to study. As my practice continued, my portfolio grew.

Despite frequent travel and high people contact, I often withdrew to be with the Father and write. And one evening after returning from a trip, a gift was waiting at my desk: a dead cicada in a baggie—courtesy of Matt.

Meeting a Mentor

As I journeyed into the creative call, God inserted a key relationship: Marge Malwitz, who became my arts-in-mission mentor. As the spring mission conference circuit began, I visited Marge's church, supporting me since 1997. Marge and Nelson Malwitz, founding members, were well-known and highly respected.

Kicking off the conference was a women's breakfast. Marge and I arrived early, with other missionaries, to set up our presentation tables in the main hall. During breakfast, we would hear briefly from several missionaries, including me. As soon as I finished my setup, I mingled with the women arriving—feeling out my audience.

In each conversation, I asked a question I'd been asking everyone connected to a church: "Do you know anything about art in mission?" No one did until this morning. To my surprise, each person replied, "Marge Malwitz"—and pointed her out to me. Across the room, a few people surrounded a woman a head taller with floppy blond hair setting up her table. Dressed in New England travel chic, complete with a colorful silk scarf, Marge looked every bit the artful, practical, and missional artist. *Kudos*, I thought. *Not an easy combination to pull off.*

While Marge set out brochures and draped her phenomenal quilts, she chatted with the people swirling around her. I walked over and waited for a lull to introduce myself. We didn't have much time before breakfast, but I knew Marge's challenge.

In any mission conference, a missionary's priority is supporting the church's goals. Time is at a premium. Set up, speak, cast vision, tell stories, share needs, flex as necessary. Camaraderie among the missionaries came second, hard-won as we run through our paces. Marge was doing her job, and I waited till she was free. When she was, I pounced, introducing myself and my ministry with Greater Europe Mission.

Across the room, a few people surrounded a woman a head taller with floppy blond hair setting up her table. Dressed in New England travel chic, complete with a colorful silk scarf, Marge looked every bit the artful, practical, and missional artist.

"In France, over there—" I pointed to my display table while Marge waved to a friend. "Do you know anything about art in mission?"

"Yes, that's what I do," she answered, handing a brochure to a child.

Stunned, I stared at the first soul I'd met who knew about arts in mission. I waited as the child asked Marge to sign the brochure. When she did and the boy ran off, I asked, "Have you ever taken artists on mission?"

"Yes, and I teach it." Marge pushed up her glasses and adjusted her scarf. I detected a New Jersey accent.

"Do you know anything about art and healing? Art therapy?" I pursued.

Marge frowned, thought a minute, and shook her head. "No, nothing."

Before we could continue, the breakfast carts rolled by, and our hosts called us to the tables. When my time came to present my ministry, I gave a quick update on France. Shifting to my new passions, I touched on the accident, depression, and my healing journey. I mentioned my investment in the arts and writing and wrapped up with the role art played in missions and healing.

As the breakfast ended, I found Marge at my table, picking up my promo materials. When she saw me approaching, she said, "Now I understand what you're talking about. Why don't you come to my studio one day? I'll tell you how art helped me with depression."

I immediately accepted Marge's offer. We chose a date, and I left the church singing—I'd met a pioneer in arts and mission. I couldn't wait to pick her brains.

Under the Walnut Tree

As I drove out of the parking lot, a magnificent walnut tree caught my attention at the end of the driveway. In full bloom, it showered petals over cars, lawn, and sidewalk, a wondrous sight. I pulled over.

As fall and winter had stripped leaves from branches, the bare trees symbolized for me grief's vulnerability. I felt emotionally naked participating in mission conferences, never knowing when tears would sabotage me. Grief didn't care who I was with or what I was doing. In any conversation, I might choke up. As an introvert, I wanted to withdraw. The emotional energy home ministry required—meeting with people and speaking to groups—depleted whatever energy grief left me. I often felt I had nothing to give. My emotional cupboard was as bare as those trees.

But this majestic walnut tree, exploding skyward in full bloom, spoke of hope and renewal. As I paused to admire it, I found myself smiling again. Spring was in riot—a season of resurrection and life. My winter of grief was ending.

Window of Hope

When studio day with Marge arrived, I hopped in my blue Toyota and drove to her neighborhood in Candlewood Lake. She welcomed me with open arms and heart, another fabulous scarf draped around her neck. In her light-dappled studio surrounded by trees and overlooking the lake, we sipped coffee and talked art, missions, and faith. After lunch, Marge pulled out boxes and bins, showing me projects—hers or others—completed, in process, or imagined. Her bookshelf was lined with books, some of which she offered me. I recorded titles as she talked, creating a reading list. We pored over her idea files and brainstormed potential projects I could try in France.

As a working artist, Marge taught art in mission at YWAM's discipleship training school in Hawaii. She traveled with her husband on short-term mission projects, creating stunning story quilts to present biblical stories. And she participated in an artist's group at her church, the Roaring Lambs. Before the day ended, Marge invited me back to her studio. If the timing worked, I could also attend the next Roaring Lambs meeting—invitations I couldn't refuse.

As the shadows lengthened, I thanked Marge for her gracious gifts of time, a meal, and inspiration. Our day birthed an enduring friendship and partnership in missions. Through my first years of art and mission, Marge encouraged me with ideas, connections, and resources. She and Nelson became prayer and financial partners. Whenever I was in Connecticut, Marge invited me for a studio day, weekend, or longer. We discovered a mutual love of the coast, lobster pots, and funky scarves.

In these life-giving studio times, Marge showered me with supplies, tips, books, ideas, and coffee. I always brought a notebook. When Marge's index finger went up, I knew a nugget was about to drop. We cooked meals with or for Nelson, their family, and friends. She generously offered her piece *Window of Hope* for this book's cover.[32] Meeting the Malwitzes and their world-changing ministries was a highlight of my year.

A Time to Throw Away

In late June, as the temperamental spring finally ceded to summer, I woke to a brilliant sun, promising us a gorgeous day. My departure was fast approaching, and God had a farewell gift for me.

Stephanie and Matt were already up and out, scouring the neighborhood for friends. As I dressed, I looked longingly out the window at the vivid colors and uncovered pool. The songbirds were singing, and the hot bugs were already in full throttle. I only had a month to enjoy it all before flying back to France's rainy, cool summer. I hated to leave and had a pile of tasks to accomplish before my year ended. My spirit drooped. The to-do list was calling, but so was this gorgeous day, and so was God.

"What are you doing here?" he asked.

"Um, about to spend time with you."

"Why don't you go outside and play? I'll call if I need you."

No child released from chores felt more joy as I bounded out the door. The day was young. The sun was rising, with healing in its

---

[32] See "A Word on the Cover Art," after Additional Resources.

wings (Malachi 4:2). Matt and Steph had already returned, having found no friends in the neighborhood.

"Pool party!" I shouted. And with whoops of delight, we jumped in and splashed for hours. There's a time for everything, including a "time to throw away" (Ecclesiastes 3:6).

When it was time to work, I finished my chores quickly and easily. Throughout the year, my goals, timeline, and schedule probably gave God a good laugh. He probably wanted to shoo me out the door more often, but I found it hard to take a day off from saving the world. This June day broke me of that toxic habit.

Now I was the one laughing. God had sent me on another treasure hunt through home ministry assignment. As I scavenged, he forged a writer, introduced me to a mentor, and healed my soul. The art therapist brought me through the last stages of grief and left me with a tool to engage the arts in mission. I had a lay certificate in counseling and one in prayer ministry. We survived 9/11.

God had set me up well for my next term in France. Now it was a time to uproot, a time to relinquish. I hated to leave and couldn't wait to return.

CHAPTER 25

Champagne and Calamity
Ronchin, France, 2002–2004

Embrace this God-life. Really embrace it, and nothing will be too much for you.
Mark 11:22–23 MSG

WHEN I REENTERED FRANCE IN 2002, I REPORTED TO the immigration office and looked for the lady with my dossier in her drawer. Instead, I found an angry mob. I stood on a corner opposite the office and stared at the mayhem. *What in the world? I'll try another time.*

I tried a week later, but the mob had grown. *Was this a strike or protest?* I approached a Moroccan woman skirting the line and asked what was happening. Her eyes never left the mob as she informed me to come no later than 5:00 a.m.—some were arriving at midnight. When the doors opened at 9:00 a.m., only a few could enter at a time. I gulped. *Seriously?*

She was right. No matter when I went, the mob didn't change, except to grow. We were in a post-9/11 world, and I was illegal. In no way did I imagine the French would deport an American, but my stress levels rose—I'd need to resolve my visa issue as soon as possible. I set my alarm for 4:30 a.m. Driving downtown in the predawn dark, I hoped the crowd would be more manageable.

The crowd was indeed smaller, calmer, and sleepier, shifting from foot to foot, some asleep on cardboard. *Better,* I thought and joined the end of the line. But weeks would pass before I succeeded in entering the building.

The lines grew as the system broke down in the wake of 9/11. They snaked around the immigration office, spilled along sidewalks, and wrapped around trees. When someone tipped me off that officers allowed only two hundred people in a day, I counted each morning on arrival. If two hundred people were ahead of me, I left and tried the next morning fifteen minutes earlier.

My strategy paid off. One morning, an officer waved me in and checked my passport. I entered another human sea of refugees, immigrants, and people like me on a temporary visa. We were in the basement, its industrial railings herding us up a double set of stairs. Desperate, numb, aged, and angry people stood, sat on the stairs, or leaned against steel gray walls. Many had children. Each had a story. My heart went out to them. Even if I was deported, I could return to my country. Not everyone had that option.

We inched up the stairs to the reception desk, where we received a ticket and waited till our number was called. While waiting, I looked for my contact, who usually sat opposite the receptionist. She had disappeared, along with her desk and my dossier.

When a frazzled clerk called my number, I approached the counter and gave her my information. Without looking up, she handed me an appointment card for a month later. I wandered out dazed. *Eight hours for an appointment?* But my quest for a visa would haunt me for the next four years.

Finding My Lane

With that despicable chore done for the moment, I refocused on ministry. La Rentrée was days away, and I had a new term to launch. How could I merge healing, dreams, the arts, writing, and poetry into a cohesive whole? I had no idea, but God must. Otherwise, he wouldn't have given me so many calls.

Caron remained my prayer partner and sounding board, and Centre Promesses provided endless networking. Sandrine connected me to artists in the network. Monique offered to work with me on poetry translation. And as I continued exchanging English conversation for French, my language skills improved. I resumed my writing practice in English and wrote my first poems in French.

I spent time leafing through the writer's market guide, tagging publishers, magazines, and journals. By now, most people were online, so I could submit from France. As I matched markets to my work, I had good success, and my publication credits grew. I searched for a writer's group, in French or English. When I was unsuccessful, I launched one in a downtown coffee shop.

But I also needed visual expression—hands-on playing with color. As a child, obsessed with fingerpainting, coloring books, and a beloved Colorforms set, I was habitually lost in color. In kindergarten, my teacher consulted my parents about my artistic streak. They chuckled and explained, "She takes after her father."

When did my father—who took me to designer showrooms and discouraged me from the arts—first notice he had an artistic daughter? What did he think? Unfortunately, it was too late to ask. But Dad's legacy—and my heavenly Father's call—compelled me. I'd taken classes during my year home and benefitted personally and professionally from art therapy sessions. But several months had elapsed without a creative outlet, and my inner artist was rattling the cage to be released. Now what?

Ateliers Attiches

My friend Anaïs invited me for watercolor workshops at her local social center in nearby Attiches. I was thrilled to have a buddy and immediately accepted. Each Monday evening, we met at her house and walked over to the center.

The imperial Jeannine, a professional artist, facilitated the workshops in oils and watercolor. I tried both. She glided among us correcting posture, brush strokes, and color choices. At the end of the year, she announced we would participate in a closing exhibition.

"But Jeannine," I protested. "I'm a novice."

"Et alors?" Jeannine sniffed. "Where is the shame in beginning?"

She had a point. As in many cultures, talent was welcome but participation expected in community art classes. Jeannine guided me in choosing the required three pieces from my portfolio and ordered me off to find (or make) frames.

How did someone like me, the illegal foreigner latecomer-to-the-arts novice, qualify for an art show in France? It was hilarious, but I wouldn't have missed it for the world. The exhibition mobilized the French with all the passion, style, and perfection they throw into any endeavor. A crew of workers (mostly husbands) descended on the center a week in advance, removing chairs and worktables, setting up folding screens and room dividers to hang artwork.

Jeannine ordered finger foods, soft drinks, and champagne. At the *vernissage* (opening night), warm temps prompted us to open doors and windows. The town filed in, and a pleasant buzz spread through the room, no doubt helped by the bubbly. Outside the windows, roses in full bloom perfumed the air, intoxicating us further.

We might have been in a Paris gallery for the attention and verve with which the French uncorked the champagne and strolled among our offerings. I've now exhibited in several unorthodox venues (including in the rubble of an earthquake-ravaged city). But I'm not sure any surpassed my first exhibit in Attiches, a remote corner of the world, with the passionate French.

Wasting Time

I signed up for a second painting class at a local adult education center. The beginner classes were full, so I studied a detailed brochure for an alternative. With its fine print and unfamiliar arts vocabulary, the brochure baffled me. I studied "Experiments with Mixed Media," which sounded feasible. Hoping for the best, I signed up and landed in a class far too advanced for me.

My classmates were skilled artists looking for new challenges in their work. I didn't even know how to hold a pencil. Hopelessly lost—in language and technique—I nevertheless felt like a kid in a candy store.

The instructor, a professional artist with big hair and oversized red glasses, quickly realized I was floundering. She sidled up to me at timely moments with a whispered instruction or some tool drawn from a hidden pocket in her voluminous clothing. Another classmate, noticing my language limitations, sat next to me to translate. With their support, I managed to finish the yearlong course and produce some credible work.

I hadn't counted on homework assignments, which meant time, space, and finding art supply stores. Feeling slightly guilty (was this even ministry?), I cleared my calendar and set up a table in a living room corner. To learn art vocabulary, I placed a pocket dictionary on the table. If the dictionary failed me, I took my materials list to the art store and showed it to a clerk. For inspiration, I studied art books—dictionary in hand—and deconstructed language and technique.

One Saturday (prime ministry time), I ran into Lille's art store to pick up some supplies but forgot one item. As I drove back, struggling with guilt and frustration, I sighed.

"I feel like I'm wasting time," I lamented.

God answered swiftly: "You've wasted enough time already."

Remembering my June morning lesson back in Hamden, I smiled. There's a time to throw away, and learning curves certainly qualify. I drove on. Now was a time to explore the arts and see where they led, even if I forgot things, detoured down rabbit trails, or hit a dead end.

I released the artistic spirit I'd bottled up for decades and played with abandon. Energy, creativity, and imagination skyrocketed. It wasn't efficient, but it was necessary.

Art supply stores became my playgrounds. If I didn't need anything, I'd browse for inspiration. My Friday afternoon art classes became the highlight of my week. Giddy as a kindergartner, I hurried downtown and up the five flights of a curving stairwell to our studio. I found my buddy, Perrine, and we giggled our way through classes. Before the year was out, Perrine and I talked about spiritual life and discovered we had both recently lost our fathers.

As I plugged into the local art scene, I enjoyed talking with artists. We understood one another. Our conversations were thought-provoking, and we relished sharing our creative endeavors. I picked up some art jargon, styles, and techniques. I was becoming an artist. And as C. S. Lewis shares in his book by the same title, I was "surprised by joy." How had I lived without it?

Art in Mission

As I cultivated the arts and imagination, my art practice broadened into worship and intercession. My spiritual discernment increased. By nature highly perceptive and sensitive, traits often viewed negatively, my thinking reversed when God affirmed, "I made you that way." It was his design—wiring he chose to fit me for the arts as well as for healing ministry.

Until this season, it never occurred to me (or anyone else in my world) to combine arts and mission, let alone healing. Before the current creative age took hold with the internet, the arts were largely ignored in the Protestant Church, except for worship music. I wondered if there were any Christian artist groups in my city and began investigating. Though I found none, a global movement was underway.

As the arts and writing dominated my ministry, I wondered how GEM and my donors would react. If they didn't support the new direction, I could lose financial support. With the recent formation of the European Union (EU), the French franc converted to the euro. I lost a sizeable chunk of finances in the exchange rate. What if I lost more?

For all I knew, God was leading me out of mission work into arts and writing. But whatever the cost, financial or otherwise, I couldn't turn back. To relinquish the energy, passion, and joy I now felt was unthinkable.

God quickly brought resolution. GEM's president and his wife, Ted and Lynn Noble, paid our team a visit and stopped by my apartment for coffee. I shared my heart with them, and Ted's reply came as a tonic: "Block time on your calendar to pursue the arts and writing. Consider it your first priority in ministry." Lynn nodded vigorously, her searching eyes gauging my response. With no hint of doubt or hesitation seeping from them, perhaps they understood better than me the importance of these calls.

GEM had no formal arts ministry, but the Nobles encouraged me to seek other artists in the mission family. At the least, we could encourage one another. Maybe a new ministry would birth through us.

Acting on their words, I spoke with the Moores and Pilches. With their blessing, I withdrew from the English classes and other activities as I added artistic ones. I continued with my art classes and online writing courses and researched ministries on the internet. To broaden my budding network, I attended arts conferences in Paris and Belgium, looking for Lille connections. I was astonished to find more pastors, theologians, and missionaries attending these conferences than artists. The tide was rising for art in the church, and God was positioning the leaders.

As Marge Malwitz networked in her world, she connected me to Geinene Carson with Operation Mobilization (OM). Geinene had worked in OM's Austria field for three years as an artist and was now back in the States. Based in OM USA's home office in Atlanta, Georgia, Geinene was mobilizing recruits and observed a trend. Whenever she mentioned her work as an artist, other artists asked if they, too, could work cross-culturally. OM ArtsLink birthed as Geinene organized and led these artists for short-term projects overseas to find out for themselves.[33]

---

[33] OM ArtsLink grew into OM Arts, recently renamed Inspiro Arts Alliance, a global network of artists of all disciplines. See https://inspiroartsalliance.org/.

I was eager to see what Geinene did on the ground. We planned an outreach in Lille for the following year but had to cancel. Storm clouds were on the horizon. The threat of war in Iraq was growing, along with anti-American sentiment. Within weeks, the climate in France flipped from anxious to outraged. I still didn't have a visa, and the euro conversion was wreaking havoc with my finances. Would I have to leave France?

> **The threat of war in Iraq was growing, along with anti-American sentiment. Within weeks, the climate in France flipped from anxious to outraged. I still didn't have a visa, and the euro conversion was wreaking havoc with my finances. Would I have to leave France?**

A Perfect Storm

Now a trip to the immigration office was a nightmare. The American embassy warned Americans to avoid crowds as hostilities increased. They didn't mention the immigration office and the angry mob I had to enter each month. The media wasn't reporting it except for images of police officers escorting illegal foreigners to an airplane. *Lord, I'm not sure I can handle this.*

More clouds gathered. In 2004, the Moores were called to lead GEM's work in Canada, which meant losing dear friends, my prayer partner, and our team leader. A year later, the Pilches announced their departure for family reasons. Our team went into crisis. A couple from the North Paris team was moving up from Paris to work with the Pilches. Now what did they do? Two short-term workers were due to arrive in September—should we cancel their placement? As senior member of the Lille team, I was the default leader to sort it out.

When the new people arrived, we regrouped and stumbled through the fall season. We met weekly for prayer and planning. What ministries did we sacrifice, continue, or create? Did anyone want to bail? Did we need to relocate?

While working to establish a healthy team, I doggedly pursued the arts, writing, and healing ministries. Torrents de Vie resumed, along with Tables Ouvertes. But I felt myself sliding toward depression—derailed by the team crisis, finances, the mob, and visa battles. With so much loss over three years, I couldn't grieve fast enough. Joy was slipping away.

While we floundered in the wind and the waves, the storm broke: I was deported.

CHAPTER 26

Making an Omelette

Ronchin, France, 2004–2006

You can't make an omelette without breaking the eggs.
French postcard

WHEN I RECEIVED THE LETTER "INVITING ME TO leave the country as soon as possible," I drove immediately to the address listed. Mercifully, this office was on the other side of Lille in a quiet neighborhood—no long lines, no mob. I plopped the letter in front of the receptionist, who called a clerk, who ushered me into his office within minutes. When he read the letter, he rolled his eyes.

"Why would France deport an American? We'll straighten this out," he assured me. "Fill out these forms and call for an appointment when you're finished."

I took the forms home, completed them, and asked Sylvie to accompany me to my next appointment. I needed moral support. And a native speaker would catch nuances and argue better in French. We brainstormed as we drove to the immigration office, prayed before entering, and waited for my interview.

When a clerk called my name, Sylvie and I followed him through a warren of corridors and closed doors until he stopped at one. Ushering us into a bare beige cubicle, he pointed to two chairs for us and sat behind a nondescript desk. As he thumbed through my file, Sylvie and I exchanged glances and waited.

To his first question, Sylvie erupted with gusto, peppering him with her own questions and commentary. She insisted the ridiculous matter be dismissed. The impassive clerk intoned a litany of *nons*, and I slumped in my chair.

Despite Sylvie's valiant efforts, we'd pry no more sympathy, commitments, or information from him. With a vigorous thump, he timestamped my dossier and assured me someone would call soon. I reminded him of my thirty-day deadline, which he waved away as a trifle.

> When I received the letter "inviting me to leave the country as soon as possible," I drove immediately to the immigration office.

Disheartened, we left the office and drove home. After dropping Sylvie off, I drove back to my apartment and flopped on the couch. Now what? We'd just received the runaround, and I had no confidence in the immigration system. *When I am afraid, I put my trust in you* (Psalm 56:3).

Dead End

A second letter arrived within two weeks: appeal denied. I phoned Howard, who alerted the church, and we gathered to pray and brainstorm. One couple offered to contact their neighbor, a government representative (equivalent to a congressman) who might be willing to intervene.

As they pursued that possibility, I tracked the news. America was now at war with Iraq, and France continued to crack down on illegal aliens. Police escorted more and more illegals to planes in handcuffs. Would I survive the political fallout?

The congressman's efforts failed, and my deadline to leave expired. My French friends grew nervous. The *gendarmes* would have no mercy, they warned, and visions of handcuffs danced in my head. Reluctantly, I booked a flight—for another month out. I hated to leave before Christmas—maybe my last in France. I laid low, a clandestine alien, hoping authorities would be distracted by the year-end holidays. But the holidays were bittersweet, punctuated with painful goodbyes, a precursor of things to come.

By the grace of God, I escaped detection. January arrived all too soon, and with it, my departure date. I packed my bags, wondering what to take, what to leave, and if I'd return. On a dismal night of torrential rain, heartsick and battling bronchitis, I locked the apartment and left.

Howard and Caron picked me up and dropped me off at a French friend's home. She would drive me to the airport in the morning. I felt like a fugitive fleeing under cover of darkness. My friend plied me with tea and sympathy and woke me early for the morning flight—one filled with questions, prayers, and tears.

Pivot

In the States, my sister scooped me up with hugs and her famous chicken noodle soup. We talked, cried, and prayed as I recovered from bronchitis and jet lag. Then I steeled myself for another tedious visa application process. After completing the paperwork, I mailed it with prayers for favor and waited for the French embassy to respond.

When the call came for an interview, I set out on a frigid morning in late January, commuting in and out of New York City to present myself. Then another wait began. Having done everything I could, I now relied on God to open or shut the French door. *My times are in your hands, Lord* (Psalm 31:15).

While waiting, I occupied myself with two activities. I needed some psychological sunshine after the stress and tension of the previous months. Poetry would do it. I signed up for an online course and thoroughly enjoyed myself. I also followed up with Geinene Carson to explore OM ArtsLink. We had communicated enough to know our visions for the arts overlapped.

As a trained fine artist, Geinene had already led teams of artists into several European countries. The trips accomplished two purposes. They inspired artists to serve God with their creative gifts. And they demonstrated to OM field leaders and local churches how the arts could be harnessed to support worship and outreach.

My training was limited and informal, but I had years of field experience, including leading short-term teams. I was actively engaged in reaching out to local artists and facilitating art events in local venues. My networks in Christian arts ministries extended to Paris, Brussels, and beyond.

OM ArtsLink relied on personal relationships and word of mouth to form teams and short-term projects. As a global agency, OM served in over one hundred countries, from rural villages to urban centers. Whether I reentered France or remained States based, I could coordinate with Geinene in organizing short-term trips for artists wherever we were invited. And the invitations were tantalizing. From all over the world, requests arrived for art classes, workshops, exhibits, and murals in hospitals and orphanages.

But I hoped to remain in Europe. I'd invested twelve years in France, and it had become home. If I obtained a visa, I could return and partner with Geinene to develop a base in Lille to launch European artists into mission. We could bring OM ArtsLink to the next level as a pioneering movement.

Our next step was to meet. I flew to Atlanta and met Geinene and her supervisor at OM USA's headquarters. The meetings went well, and I had a tour of the facility, which included a bookstore. I noticed a book on dreams and bought it.

In the evening, processing what I'd learned, a stab of grief hit me at the thought of leaving France. My heart said yes, but my mind balked. If I moved back to the States, my financial support could evaporate. What if I moved only to lose support, need a job, and sacrifice my dream of arts ministry? But if the embassy denied me a visa, what choice did I have?

With the recent formation of the EU, anyone denied a visa in one participating country would be denied in the others. Unless

France approved my visa application, OM ArtsLink was the last arts ministry option I knew—the only one of its kind.

Before falling asleep, I read the dream book a bit, asking God to counsel me in the night. He responded with a dream that indicated he would be with me, whichever fork in the road I chose. In the morning, I flew back to Hamden, assuring Geinene I'd be in touch with her soon.

I called my GEM France field director. Could I be seconded (loaned) to OM ArtsLink while remaining with GEM? I wasn't ready to cut ties with an agency I loved. And the potential was enormous to bring a theology of arts to GEM through their seminaries and Bible institutes.

As I talked over my situation with friends, donors, and allies, reactions were mixed but favorable. A familiar intuition overshadowed the financial risk: if I refused, my life would be diminished. I called Geinene. With her agreement, I applied to join OM on loan from GEM.

Breaking Eggs

Confirmations came in rapid succession—including a letter from the French embassy denying my visa application. The door to France and EU countries closed. But God had already opened a new one.

In May I reentered France as a tourist, which allowed me to stay for three months without a visa. Whether or not that was legal, I hoped to slip in and out before anyone noticed. Three months would give me enough time to sell the car, pack my belongings, and close out the apartment—the practical side of moving. The emotional side would be another matter. How does one end life in another country after twelve years?

I prepared a to-do list, which grew to frightening proportions with plenty of unknowns. In the evenings, I pored over contracts and estimates in French legalese to figure out international shipping. *How much did a container hold? Did I need one? To what address do*

I ship? I reviewed my lease. *What would it cost to break it? Should I sublet till it expires?*

On a second list, I jotted names of people with whom I wanted to close well—friends, neighbors, teammates, ministry partners, the churches, my Centre Promesses crowd, even some shopkeepers. A third list covered my favorite places—museums, canal walks, and the park in Croix, which had saved my sanity in recent years. I'd wander the ancient cobblestones of Vieux Lille (Old Lille), arriving at the Grande Place, with its starburst of pedestrian streets filled with shops and cafés. Would I have time for a day in Paris or England?

My brain whirred in overdrive as the pressure mounted daily on logistics—what to pack, what to sell, what to ship, and when. I completed my application to OM, requested temporary accommodations, and arranged to ship my goods to a storage unit.

The work staggered me, but I trusted the transition to go smoothly. God was orchestrating a change I never imagined and wouldn't have chosen. As much as I hated surrendering life in France, I would gain better alignment with my callings, passions, and gifts. My English was now sloppy and outdated. I needed to sharpen it for writing. Although I underestimated the emotional wallop, I knew it was a healthy move.

A Les Cèdres buddy now living in Norway flew down to say goodbye—a welcome diversion. I showed off the city, with its Flemish architecture, cathedral spires, and star-shaped citadel. We ate crêpes in Meert's wondrous nineteenth-century tea salon and visited an abbey boutique. I said goodbye to each place, hoping to see it again one day.

When she left, I took the train to Grenoble, where one of my dearest French friends had moved with her family. On a blistering July day, we sheltered in the cool caves of the Chartreuse Abbey—on my bucket list for some years.

Thankfully, France slows considerably in spring and summer. In June, the schools closed, and our ministry activities stopped. I said goodbye to my students and turned the writer's group over to a colleague. Other ministries would carry on without me. By July, I had checked off more items on my list than I expected.

The great purge began. I sold, junked, or donated as much as possible. As I packed the rest, I paused each day to swim at the pool, grab lunch with friends, or walk a favorite park. I second-guessed myself continually—*Am I making the right decision?*

As I packed a bookshelf one morning, a postcard fluttered to the floor. I picked it up and chuckled—an image of broken eggs with a French proverb: "You can't make an omelette without breaking the eggs." *Got it, Lord. To pursue the arts, I'll have to break some eggs.*

I didn't expect my heart to break too. I propped the postcard on the shelf as a reminder of my goal and continued to dismantle my life in France.

Au Revoir, La France

I registered for one more weekend at a nearby retreat center I frequented. Its formidable seminary building rose from the grounds—an intimidating, if neglected, presence. I stared up at it, a symbol of the daunting transition I faced, and entered. With twenty acres of parks, gardens, and horse pastures, it proved an ideal place to prepare spiritually.

Jesuit priests operated the center. I happened to sit next to one for the first time at the retreat's last meal. The irony didn't escape me. This was the first Jesuit I had conversed with since Uncle Leo, as I shared with this young priest. He looked pleased.

"Is this brother still alive?" he asked.

"No," I replied, "but isn't it striking that I sit next to you—a Jesuit priest—as I close my life in France? When my Jesuit uncle introduced me to missional life? It's like bookends, no?"

The impenetrable question hung between us. What message had God tucked into this chance encounter? Generally, the French tackle such questions with relish but not tonight. We fell into silence until someone passed the carrots, and conversation resumed.

But it felt like bookends to me—a spiritual closing, a click in my spirit like Uncle Leo's watch case. As dinner ended, I rose from the table fully satisfied by the meal, the conversation, and the sound of my assignment in France clicking to a close.

By August, the country practically shut down. I bought a few last art supplies from my preferred art store and gave away most of my artwork. Every available evening, I sat on my balcony with the geraniums, watching rainbows and hot air balloons. Under the battleship clouds, swallows swooped back and forth to the linden tree, now as tall as my balcony. Though it finally afforded me the shade and privacy I desired, it blocked my view—another indication it was time to move on.

Two weeks before my departure, I surrendered the apartment and moved in with colleagues Leroy and Debbie Zumack. A few days later, I sold my car. On my last Sunday in church, I read a farewell poem I'd written, sobbing my way through it. I'm not sure a day passed in my last weeks when I didn't cry. Each goodbye was painful, each carton packed with emotions. As a remarkable chapter ended, I was physically and emotionally wrecked. So many goodbyes. So many logistics.

The Zumacks drove me to the train station, and I rode the bullet train south out of Lille. I stared out the window at the coal slags, red poppies, and yellow *colza* fields carpeting the rolling green hills. Dotting the landscape were the trenches, bunkers, and cemeteries with white crosses of World War I. I memorized it all.

I'd miss my international world—French, Belgian, Dutch, Moroccan, Italian, German, British. No more *moules et frites* at the Braderie or *pain au chocolate* from Paul's bakery. No more ferry rides across the English Channel for a British day. I'd miss the Algerian bookstore, serving tea and biscuits. Maybe I'd see Bruges again, Belgium's Venice, for Leonidas chocolates and lace—OM worked in Belgium.

We curved around the distinctive spire of Senlis's cathedral, and the Paris skyline appeared. Pastoral farmlands morphed into urban sprawl. Planes landed and departed over Roissy Charles de Gaulle Airport. A few hours later, I boarded one, fastened my seat belt, and flew into the next adventure. Life as I'd known it for twelve years was over. It was time to make an omelette.

Epilogue

Florida, November 2021

Dear friend, I pray that you may enjoy good health and that all may go well with you, even as your soul is getting along well.

3 John 2

TWENTY-FOUR YEARS LATER, THIS GIRL MOVED TO Florida and stumbled across an old letter. I turned it into a manuscript, which grew into a book and left home to find you. Now that you've met, I hope *Collision* introduced you to its true author and a few new ideas on healing.

In 1985, when I prayed for healing in that emergency room, I never imagined God would answer with a twelve-year journey that included art, writing, dreams, and missions. And that's just the external story.

God's definition of healing went exponentially beyond mine—into transformation, the internal story. I remain healed. My health and energy continually improved over the years, and I have been virtually affliction free for over two decades.

God conceived my story before the world's foundations and releases it as he chooses (Ephesians 1:4). I've not stopped sharing it around the world, with countless people in dozens of countries. In planes, hallways, and at kitchen tables, I speak when prompted—"Let me tell you what happened to me . . ."

As I share, many have asked for and received healing prayer. Many acknowledge a need to forgive. In praying with them, I developed my own Seven Steps to Forgiveness, distilling the lessons of years.

As God healed my inner story, he released joy, creativity, calls, and vocation. When I made a costly mistake at the immigration office, God redeemed it, catapulting me into the most fruitful period of my life and ministry. Gifts and ministries I never anticipated became my life's work. For over twenty years, I've enjoyed serving with and reaching out to artists, cultivating their spiritual and creative lives.

The kingdom collision that reversed the effects of a car accident operated through the ministry of gifted individuals. God meticulously placed them at a critical crossroads in my journey—in the Vermont mountains, where my healing journey both ended and expanded. My profound gratitude for each individual and ministry mentioned here runs second only to God, who eclipses all.

Dr. Mullen included my story in his book, *Emotionally Free.*[34] In 2009, a French friend called to ask if I'd talk to a friend—Dr. Craig Keener, a seminary professor at Palmer Seminary in Pennsylvania. Dr. Keener contacted me shortly after to verify my story for inclusion in a book on miracles.

I'm aware my story is unusual. God wrote a unique script. Some chapters may be particular to the calls and gifts he placed in me. But while my story is unique, God's transformational work in us is universal.

Each reader's healing journey will likewise be unique. Not everyone finds healing in this life, but anyone can live an epic story within God's story, as Paul did despite his affliction. For God's tale is one of eternal hope, reconciliation, and redemption. He invites us to participate in his divine nature, giving us everything we need for a godly life, including great and precious promises. We can escape

---

[34] Available from Dr. Grant Mullen, www.drgrantmullen.com or Amazon.

"the corruption in the world caused by evil desires" (2 Peter 1:4). We can be heroes, even by accident.

The mystery of healing continues. I have new questions but have discovered some principles:

- I might not be the instrument of God's healing. It took me twelve years to connect with Dr. Mullen. When he prayed, I received healing. Others who had prayed weren't necessarily less spiritual, but they weren't God's choice, nor was I ready. The opposite also applies. I might pray for someone who receives healing after others had already prayed who were no less spiritual than me.
- Timing belongs to God. Whether during a prayer session or years later, answers await an appointed time.[35] God timed my visit to Nadine with Yvonne's. Dr. Mullen, delayed at the border, arrived on time for God's purposes. When God doesn't appear to heal, it may be a matter of time.
- Jesus includes deliverance in commissioning his followers.[36] If we ignore deliverance, we may miss healing. If we focus too much on deliverance, we might miss the inner healing God desires.
- Every situation is unique. When I pray with the sick, some receive healing, some don't. While encouraging me to persevere, God reminds me he is sovereign.
- We like speed. When we consult our human physicians and hear their diagnoses, we often ask, "Do you have a pill for that?" Expecting speedy results from the Great Physician is like expecting French cuisine at a fast-food chain. When we call on God for healing, we are wise to prepare for a journey. The course of treatment he prescribes might take twelve years.
- We persevere until God says to stop.

---

[35] Habakkuk 2:3; Galatians 4:4–5; Psalm 139:16
[36] Luke 9:1–4; 10:1–19; Mark 16:17–18

Our Great Physician knew how to prepare and position me for an appointed hour of healing—during one conference, bathed in prayer and worship in Vermont. Why didn't God convict me of sin earlier? Why did it take twelve years? I'll save that story for another book.

Whatever your journey, my heart's desire is John's prayer: that you may enjoy good health, that all may go well with you, even in your soul. May you mine the treasures hidden in the darkest passages. When God is silent or human answers don't satisfy, persevere like Job. If this story brings you hope and healing, pass the word. There is a God who heals—but not always as we expect. His name is Jehovah-Rapha.

Healing Vision Statement

The LORD be exalted, who delights in the well-being of his servant.

Psalm 35:27

OUR FIRST HEALING IS RECONCILIATION WITH THE Father, who is reconciling all things to himself.[37] Reconciled through Jesus, we discover he is also Jehovah-Rapha, the Lord who heals.[38] Healing is consistent with God's character, revealed in his names, incarnated in Jesus Christ.

I. Names of God

- *Elohim*—our creator (Genesis 1:1)
- *Jehovah-Rapha*—the LORD who heals (Exodus 15:26)
- *Jehovah-Shammah*—the LORD is there (Ezekiel 48:35), always present to us in affliction (Hebrews 13:5; Romans 8:38–39)
- *El Roi*—the God who sees (Genesis 16:13) all our pain, suffering, and wounds and will one day render justice
- *Jehovah-Mekoddishkem*—the LORD who sanctifies, sets us apart, and purifies us (Exodus 31:13; Leviticus 20:8)

II. Incarnation

Jesus, the resurrection and the life, came that we might experience abundant life.[39] Healing was integral to his ministry; he treated

---

[37] Colossians 1:20
[38] Exodus 15:26; Romans 5:1
[39] John 10:10; John 11:25–26

sickness as an enemy.[40] Although he responded to the faith of anyone seeking healing, he didn't require it; sometimes, others' faith in Jesus moved him to heal.[41] He commissioned his apostles, disciples, and followers to preach the gospel and to heal,[42] affirming that his followers would do greater works than he did.[43]

III. God's Unchanging Nature

- Jesus Christ is the same yesterday, today, and forever.[44] Jehovah-Rapha still heals and desires to heal—he instructs his followers to heal the sick. Since Jesus leaves instructions in case of sickness, we can assume it's normally his will to heal.[45]
- Jesus heals out of compassion, a man of sorrows, acquainted with grief, familiar with pain and suffering. He is gracious, compassionate, and merciful.[46]
- Jesus heals according to his sovereign purposes in redemption, to restore what Adam and Eve lost in the garden or what the enemy has stolen, killed, or destroyed.[47]
- He is our Great High Priest who empathizes with us and invites us to ask for healing, to approach him when we need mercy and grace.[48]

In his ongoing work of redemption and transformation, the Father heals and restores us from the effects of Adam and Eve's choice in Eden—including physical, spiritual, and emotional healings.

---

[40] Acts 10:38
[41] Mark 3:5; 5:1–9; 6:5–6; 7:24–30; 9:20–24; Psalm 147:3; Acts 3:1–9
[42] Matthew 10:7–8; Luke 9:1–2; Luke 10:1–19; Mark 16:17–18
[43] John 14:12
[44] Hebrews 13:8
[45] James 5:14–16
[46] Isaiah 53:3; Psalm 145:8
[47] Genesis 3; John 10:10
[48] Hebrews 4:15–16

A Healing Lifestyle

*"Make level paths for your feet," so that the lame may not
be disabled, but rather healed.*
Hebrews 12:13

WE HONOR GOD BY HONORING OUR BODIES[49] AND cultivating a healthy lifestyle. We dishonor God by presuming on his grace for healing while ignoring self-care and health principles.

Before seeking any healing course of action, it's wise to consult God first[50] and follow the instructions in James 5:14–16. Since James connects confession with healing, we exam ourselves before God and others.

After prayer, it's appropriate to pursue healing with wisdom and common sense. We may explore natural avenues, medical care, and counseling. Pursuing healing simultaneously through prayer ministry and doctors is not a lack of faith. One pursuit is not more spiritual than the other. If traditional medicine and counseling don't bring healing, we explore spiritual roots.

When God doesn't appear to heal, it may be a matter of timing. Rather than guess or assume that God won't heal, we ask, like Paul did, and listen and wait for answers.[51] God may reveal the affliction's purpose or affirm his power to sustain us, as he did with Paul. As we ask for words, revelation, or understanding, perhaps we gain a

---

[49] 1 Corinthians 6:20
[50] 2 Kings 1:1–4
[51] 2 Corinthians 12:8–10

key insight that unlocks healing. Or, like Paul, God doesn't heal but gives us a word, redeems our affliction, and we have peace.

Sometimes God doesn't heal all at once.[52] Healing can come through the divine and miraculous or through human instrument; through spiritual gifts and prayer or medical intervention; or in any combination God chooses. Each healing is unique. Jesus chooses the time, place, people, gifts, and circumstances.

Healing doesn't depend only on our faith, but faith plays a critical role. It pleases God and stirs him to act.[53] With faith, we collaborate with God in our healing. If we have no faith for healing, we can pray, "I do believe. Help my unbelief" (Mark 9:24 NASB).

Lack of healing may indicate unresolved sin—personal, corporate, or national—or not, or satanic attack.[54] Medicating physical symptoms for spiritual sickness will be ineffective, as will assuming spiritual disease without testing the spirits.

In everything, exercise discernment to avoid spiritual counterfeits.

---

[52] 2 Kings 5; Mark 8:23–25
[53] Mark 7:24–30
[54] John 9:1–3; Job 1–2

A Word on the Cover Art

*To all who are passionately dedicated to the search for new
"epiphanies" of beauty so that through their creative work
as artists they may offer these as gifts to the world.*[55]
—Pope John Paul II

"WINDOW OF HOPE" IS ONE IN A SERIES OF ORIGINAL
quilt designs created by Marge Malwitz. In 2007, the
quilts traveled to Rwanda for healing and reconciliation workshops following the 1994 genocide. Sponsored by World
Relief, the workshops facilitated a visual experience, inviting survivors to reconcile their stories under the cross of Christ.

I sat in Marge's studio as she showed me the invitation she'd
received to help facilitate the workshops. While wondering what to
offer genocide survivors, Marge mined her own story for life lessons
that might connect. Through prayer, meditation, and research, she
found her theme and began playing with format, materials, and
design. As Marge worked through the creative process, four quilts
emerged: two from her experience with depression and two after
hearing a Rwandan's testimony.

Design inspiration came from the book *Land of a Thousand
Hills*[56] and a friend's photos of Rwanda's hills. After receiving African
fabric scraps from a visiting World Relief missionary, Marge added

---

[55] Pope John Paul II, Letter of His Holiness Pope John Paul II to Artists,
(Boston: Pauline Books & Media, 1999).
[56] Rosamond Halsey Carr, *Land of a Thousand Hills: My Life in Rwanda*
(New York: Plume, the Penguin Group, 2000).

them to other scraps from her global travels and created her quilts in the States. On arrival in Rwanda, she shopped at a local market for fabrics to use in the workshops following her presentations.

Each quilt told God's story of reconciliation as he might visually tell it to Rwandans. The quilts provoked deep responses, prompting some survivors to begin their journeys back to wholeness. As trainers replicated what they learned, the workshops spread across the country. Marge tells the story in her blog series, "Rwanda."[57]

When the quilts returned, they found a home in a chapel in the Jericho Partnership, a ministry serving at-risk youth in Danbury, Connecticut. On my next visit, Marge invited me to see them.

When I saw "Window of Hope," something resounded in my spirit. With its dominant cross, the quilt graphically proclaimed hope's origin. Sparkling blue thread and a trio of orange flames symbolized the Spirit. They led the eye from the cross to a patch of blue sky in the upper right quadrant—a window of hope. Although I saw the quilt a decade after my healing, it captivated me.

Marge then stunned me by offering a giclee print of one of the designs. I immediately chose "Window of Hope." Like Marge, I had experienced depression. In the darkness, we both found windows of hope in God's Word, through which we escaped. In particular, Job stirred us: "But he knows the way that I take; when he has tested me, I will come forth as gold" (Job 23:10). "Though he slay me, yet will I hope in him" (Job 13:15).

As God birthed *Collision*, "Window of Hope" flashed through my mind. Now framed, it hangs in my bedroom, one of my first sights on waking. Though not a literal, visual expression of the car accident that launched my journey, my external story, "Window of Hope" completely captures my internal story—a collision between the kingdom of darkness and the kingdom of light. What better image to choose for *Collision* than the cross?

---

[57] Marge Malwitz, "Rwanda," (blog posts), March, April, May 2010, https://margemalwitz.blogspot.com/search/label/Rwanda.

Resources

Visit my website for additional resources, or explore this sampling.

- Christian Healing Ministries: https://www.christianhealingmin.org/
- Desert Streams/Living Waters, Andy Comisky: www.desertstream.org
- Freedom in Christ Ministries: www.ficm.org
- Ministries of Pastoral Care: https://ministriesofpastoralcare.com/
- Dr. Grant Mullen: www.drgrantmullen.com
- Andrew Murray, *Divine Healing*: available on Amazon
- Order of St. Luke, *A Healing Season, Devotional Study on Jesus the Healer*: available at https://osltoday.org/

Mission Agencies:

- Greater Europe Mission: https://www.gemission.org/
  - Camp of the Peaks: https://www.campdescimes.com
- Operation Mobilization:
  - OM USA: https://www.omusa.org/
  - Inspiro Arts Alliance: https://inspiroartsalliance.org/
  - OM International: https://www.om.org/en

I'd love to hear your healing journey! If you'd like to share, please contact me. If your church or ministry would like me to share my story, I'd welcome the opportunity.

- Pbutler317@gmail.com
- www.mythicmonastery.org
- FB: Patricia Butler
- IG: @mythic_monastery
- Pinterest: Mythic Monastery

If this book has helped you, would you consider writing a review to help others find hope? You can spread the word that there is a God who heals. Together we will fulfill his call to bind up the brokenhearted, proclaim freedom for the captives, and release from darkness for the prisoners (Isaiah 61:1).

Thank you!

ORDER INFORMATION

REDEMPTION
P R E S S

To order additional copies of this book, please visit
www.redemption-press.com.
Also available on Amazon.com and BarnesandNoble.com
or by calling toll-free 1-844-2REDEEM.

CPSIA information can be obtained
at www.ICGtesting.com
Printed in the USA
JSHW030853260622
27342JS00003B/17